A LIFE FOR A LIFE

THE WORLD'S MOST EVIL SERIAL KILLERS

SparkPool

Illustrated by Maurizio Campidelli
Written by Claire Sipi

Designed by Simon Parker
Edited by Alexandra Chapman

Published in 2024
First published in the UK by SparkPool Publishing
An imprint of Igloo Books Ltd
Cottage Farm, NN6 0BJ, UK
Owned by Bonnier Books
Sveavägen 56, Stockholm, Sweden

Manufactured in China. 1124 001
10 9 8 7 6 5 4 3 2 1

Library of Congress Cataloging-in-Publication
Data is available upon request.

ISBN 978-1-83795-643-2
IglooBooks.com
bonnierbooks.co.uk

CONTENTS

INTRODUCTION

The topic of serial killers is grisly and unnerving, and exploring their crimes is not for the faint-hearted. Their heinous actions destroy countless innocent lives, as well as those of their families and friends. These coldblooded killers leave a deadly trail of depraved violence in their wake, and their lack of remorse or empathy can be both chilling and frightening.

This book reveals snapshot accounts of 23 of the "worst of the worst" offenders from all four corners of the world. Some are infamous killers that you may already have heard of, and others are less well-known. Each account will tell the stories of their early lives, the motives and methods of their crimes, and how they were eventually caught, tried, and sentenced.

So, what drives someone to take lives in such a cold and casual manner? How can we ever truly understand why a serial killer is compelled to do what they do? The answer might never be certain, despite the countless studies conducted on their lives. As humans, we are driven to analyze the things we can't explain, which is why there is such a huge fascination with capital crime. With information and knowledge, we can gain an insight into the minds of these people. What they have done can never be justified. It is often found that they had a terrible start in life, but one might wonder why someone born into hardship might want to inflict pain onto others, too.

Much has been written about what causes a person to become a killer. Is someone born a killer or do they become one? Is a killer created by a combination of their intrinsic nature and their environment? This debate is ongoing. However, the fact remains that most serial killers have had chaotic and often tragic childhoods marred by years of abuse, including physical, emotional, and/or sexual. There are, however, exceptions to this statistic, as you will discover throughout this book.

Of course, the majority of abused or neglected children don't go on to become serial killers. However, it has been scientifically proven that a person's genetics and the environment that they are brought up in do affect their behavior. If a child is subjected to abuse, humiliation, or neglect, this may encourage violent behavior and a tendency to act on those feelings. Physical damage to the brain, either genetically or caused by external traumas, could also lead to personality disorders, such as paranoid schizophrenia, dissociative identity disorder, narcissism, and other antisocial disorders.

Many serial killers that have been studied exhibited certain traits in their childhoods, such as bed-wetting beyond the age of 12, starting fires, or injuring or killing small animals. Those who go on to become sexual predators have usually displayed voyeuristic tendencies in their youth, and have entertained violent or erotic sexual fantasies and enjoyed hardcore pornography. Many serial killers have had alcoholic tendencies or have been drug abusers.

An abused child will most likely become emotionally detached. They might begin to lack empathy and suffer from feelings of isolation and low self-esteem, or struggle to form meaningful relationships. The reality of their world will lead them to seek comfort in fantasies, often ones where they are in control. Eventually the boundary between fantasy and reality blurs, and this can sometimes result in violent, domineering behavior and ultimately, and tragically, lead to murder.

However, rest assured that statistically, only around one percent of murders today are committed by serial killers. Since the peak of active serial killers during the 1970s-1990s, there has been a steep decline in their presence in society. Fortunately, it is much more difficult in the present day to commit multiple murders without getting caught. This is due to better coordination between police forces and law enforcement agencies, more sophisticated DNA testing, detailed digital databases of known criminals, better surveillance in towns and cities, and stricter parole laws.

Hopefully, as technology continues to advance, and our understanding of what can cause someone to kill improves, future potential murderers will be stopped before they become rampant serial killers.

RODNEY ALCALA

SENTENCED TO DEATH · SENTENCED TO DEATH · SENTENCED TO DEATH · SENTENCED TO DEATH ·

CRIMINAL PROFILE:

Name: Rodrigo Jacques Alcala Buquor
Date of birth: August 23, 1943
Place of birth: San Antonio, Texas
Also known as: The Dating Game Killer
Victims: 8 confirmed, could be as many as 130
Convicted: Sentenced to death

THE YOUNG ALCALA

When Alcala was 8 years old, his father abandoned the family, leaving them destitute. Little detail is known about this time in his life, but it is thought the abandonment could have been the trigger for Alcala's violent behavior in later life.

He joined the US army at age 17, but he was discharged in 1964 after suffering a nervous breakdown and being diagnosed with a chronic antisocial personality disorder (ASPD).

He was displaying all of the classic traits of a sociopath; he was callously indifferent, antagonistic, manipulative, and showed no guilt or remorse for his behavior.

In 1968, Alcala graduated from UCLA with a degree in fine arts. Having never sought help for his ASPD, he was a ticking time bomb waiting to explode.

On the morning of September 25, 1968, Alcala abducted 8-year-old Tali Shapiro when she was on her way to school. He raped and beat her, but miraculously she survived the attack.

While under surveillance by the FBI, Alcala moved to New York. Using the alias John Berger, he enrolled at New York University to study film. The number of victims he amassed during this time is still unknown, but in 1971 he was recognized from the FBI list, arrested, and extradited to California for the 1968 rape and attempted murder of Shapiro.

Shapiro's family kept her from testifying, which made a rape conviction unattainable. He was released on parole in 1974, but within a couple of months he was arrested again for assaulting a 13-year-old girl, and spent two more years in prison. After his release, Alcala embarked on an escalating killing spree.

THE DATING GAME

Incredibly, even though he was a convicted child molester at the time, in September 1978 Alcala appeared on an American TV show called *The Dating Game*. The show didn't run a background check, and Alcala, or Bachelor No.1, was introduced as a successful photographer. He won a date with Cheryl Bradshaw, but when she met him, she canceled the date as he was "acting really creepy." This decision probably saved her life.

"I'm called the **'THE BANANA'** *and I look really good . . .* **PEEL ME.** *"*
- RODNEY ALCALA (ON *THE DATING GAME* TV SHOW)

METHODS AND MOTIVES

Alcala thrived on deception and lies, hiding his brutal nature behind a mask of charm and good looks. Posing as a fashion photographer, he was able to lure many of his victims with the promise of portfolios. Autopsies revealed Alcala's barbaric signature methods: he would torture his victims by strangling them to the point of unconsciousness with their own tights or shoelaces, then resuscitating them at least once before beating them to death with a blunt object. He would sometimes pose his victims' bodies postmortem and take photos of them. He also liked to take trophies from the crime scenes, such as their jewelry.

Alcala's desire for control and power was the primary driving force behind his crimes, likely stemming from a lifelong sense of abandonment.

CAPTURE AND TRIAL

Eventually, Alcala's terrifying killing spree came to an end when he was arrested on July 24, 1979 for the abduction and murder of 12-year-old Robin Samsoe, after his parole officer recognized him from a sketch of the suspect.

The police later found a receipt of Alcala's for a storage locker in Seattle, in which they found hundreds of photographs, mostly of young women, naked or in swimwear. They also found earrings that belonged to Robin Samsoe.

Alcala was convicted and sentenced to death three times for killing Samsoe, but the first two trials were overturned by appeals. 2010 saw his third trial, where he was also being tried for four other murders. Alcala chose to defend himself and, bizarrely, cross-examined himself in the third person using a different voice when he was "the attorney." He was found guilty of all five of the murders and sentenced to death.

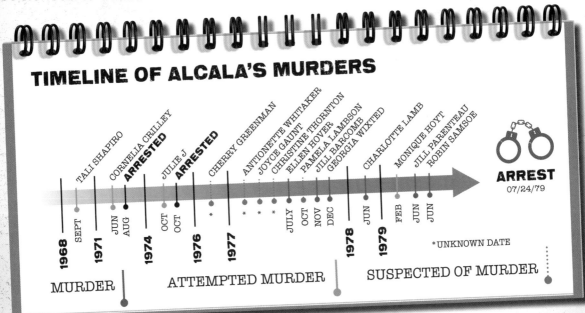

DEATH

On July 24, 2021, 77-year-old Rodney Alcala died of unspecified natural causes at a hospital in Kings County, near the Corcoran and San Quentin State Prison in California, where he had been on death row awaiting execution.

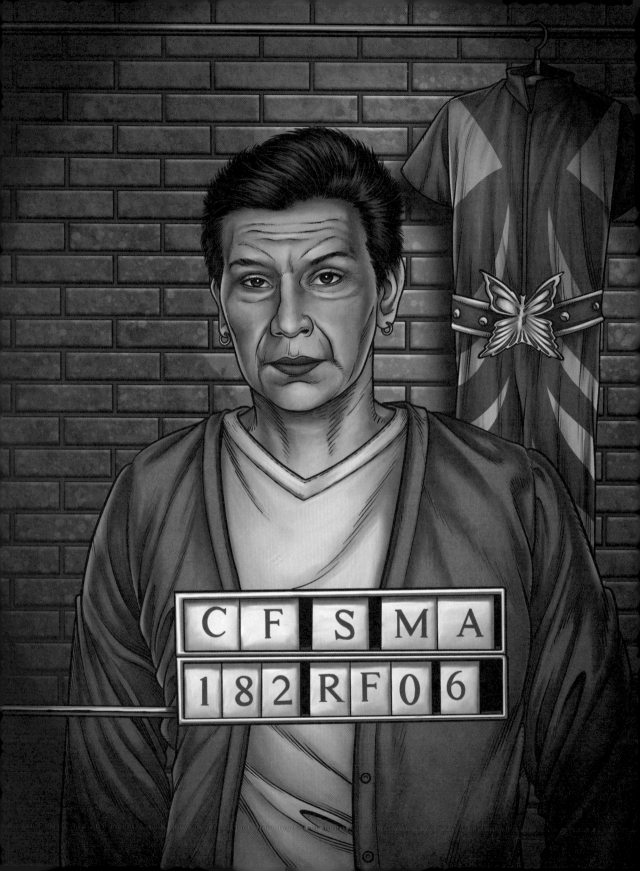

JUANA BARRAZA

759 YEARS · 759 YEARS · 759 YEARS · 759 YEARS · 759 YEARS · 759 YEARS

THE YOUNG BARRAZA

Juana Barraza was born in rural Mexico and became the country's first confirmed serial killer. Her father, a police officer, was away from home a lot with work. She was left in the care of her alcoholic mother, who was a sex worker. Regularly unsupervised, she had little schooling and never learned to read. At the age of 12, her mother reportedly gave her to one of her clients for a carton of beer, and the client proceeded to abuse her.

As soon as she could, teenage Barraza moved away to Mexico City. During the 1980s and 1990s, she had a variety of menial jobs and supplemented her earnings by stealing and selling random goods. She was a huge fan of Lucha Libre, a form of masked wrestling where the wrestlers perform acrobatic leaps off the ropes to fight their opponents. Barraza spent a lot of time socializing with the local wrestlers. She even invented a professional wrestling name for herself—"La Dama del Silencio" (The Lady of Silence)—with her own costume and mask, although it is believed that she never actually performed. During this period of her life, she is understood to have been married several times and had four children.

With a family to provide for, Barraza was desperate. It was then that she and a friend came up with a scheme to start stealing from rich, elderly women who lived alone. This was to be the dark turning point in her life, when burglary turned to murder.

"I only killed one old lady. It is not right to pin the others on me."
—JUANA BARRAZA

11

METHODS AND MOTIVES

On November 25, 2002, Barraza carried out her first murder, savagely beating and strangling 64-year-old María de la Luz González Anaya. Barraza was strong, stocky, and able to easily overpower her older, vulnerable victims. She chose her targets methodically, identifying elderly women who lived alone from a government assistance program list. Posing as a medical worker or offering to help carry groceries, Barraza would gain entry to her victims' homes, where she would murder them and then ransack the house to steal valuable keepsakes to sell or keep as mementos.

For just over three years, Barraza was able to carry out her horrific killing spree with relative ease. There was huge outrage in Mexico when sweet old abuelas (grandmothers) began to be murdered in their own homes. The police were slow to react. Corruption was rife, and they focused their search on cross-dressing prostitutes after several witnesses claimed they had seen a stocky man wearing women's clothing leaving the crime scenes. Police cars cruised the streets of Mexico City with a composite drawing of the suspected killer in their windows.

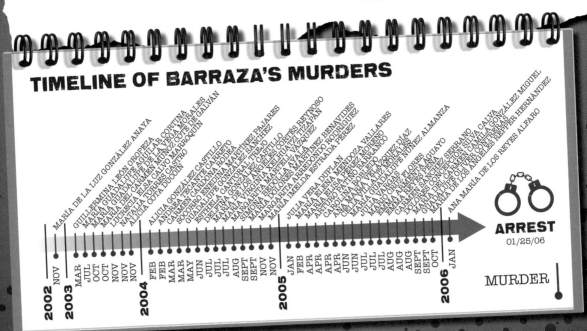

TIMELINE OF BARRAZA'S MURDERS

ARREST
01/25/06

MURDER

CAPTURE AND TRIAL

Finally, on January 25 2006, the day of Barraza's last gruesome murder, she was caught and arrested after fleeing the home of her victim, 82-year-old Ana María de los Reyes Alfaro. A neighbor named Joel Lopez had gone to visit Reyes and found the door unlocked. He entered and encountered Barraza as she was leaving. After finding Reyes dead, Lopez notified the police, and they were able to catch the killer before she disappeared into a metro station.

The police were able to link at least 10 murders to Barraza with fingerprint evidence left behind at multiple crime scenes. She insisted she wasn't the only person behind the killings, but the police didn't find any evidence of an accomplice.

In 2008, a judge declared Barraza guilty of 16 counts of first-degree murder and 12 counts of aggravated burglary. She was sentenced to 759 years in prison. She only admitted to her last victim's murder, but the prosecution alleged that she may have been responsible for as many as 40 deaths, perhaps even more.

Juana Barraza is currently incarcerated at the Santa Martha de Acatitla prison in Mexico City, where she will most likely be for the rest of her life. Eventually, she confessed that she had committed her crimes out of a sense of anger at elderly women in general, and that she believed she was helping society by killing them. She said she was never really motivated by financial gain. Her hatred was rooted in feelings toward her alcoholic mother, who had never cared for her and then subsequently abandoned her.

"With all due respect to the authorities, **THERE ARE SEVERAL OF US INVOLVED IN EXTORTION AND KILLING PEOPLE,** *so why don't the police go after the others too?"*
—JUANA BARRAZA

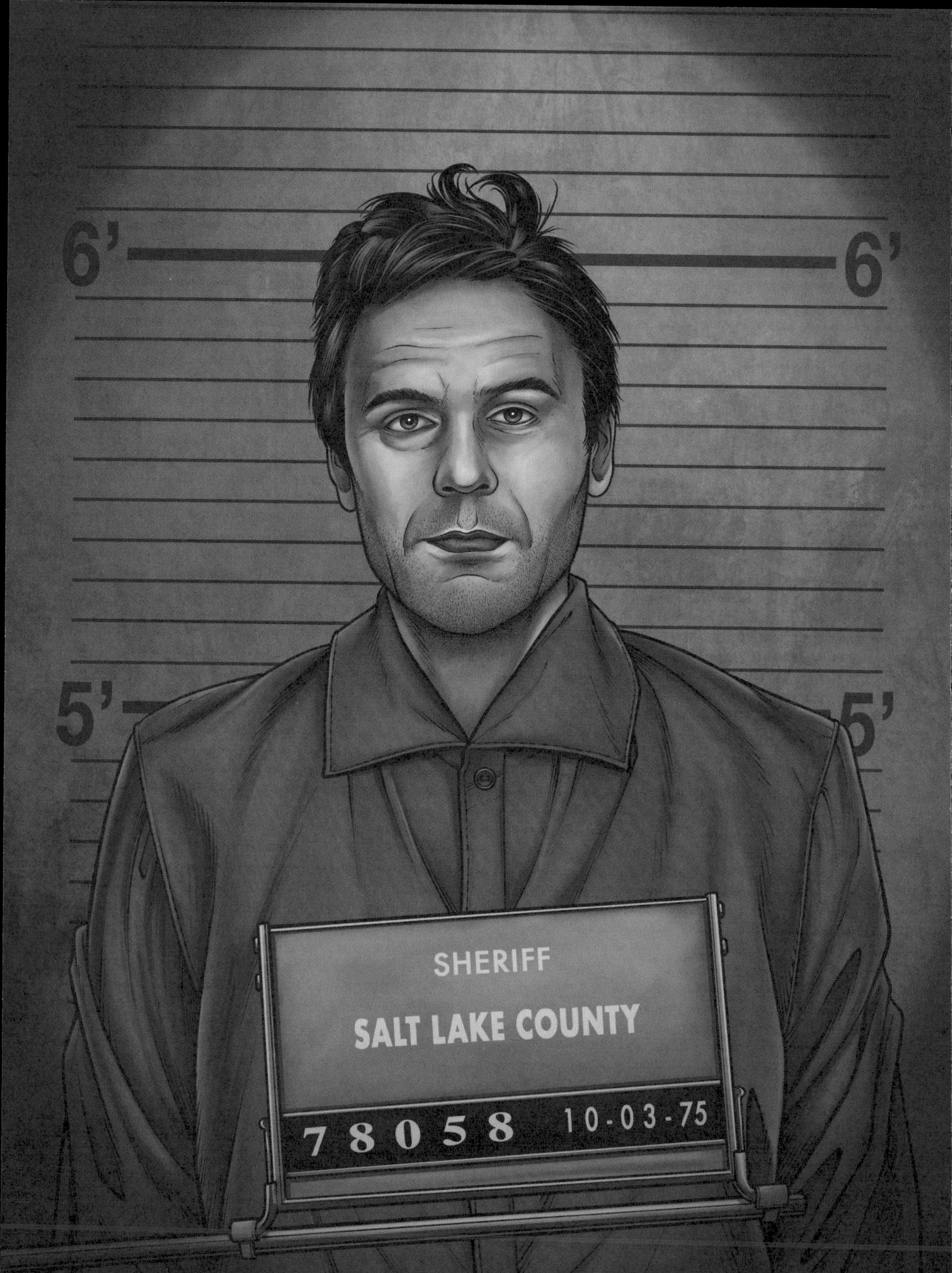
6'
6'
5'
5'
SHERIFF
SALT LAKE COUNTY
78058
10-03-75

TED BUNDY

SENTENCED TO DEATH · SENTENCED TO DEATH · SENTENCED TO DEATH · SENTENCED TO DEATH ·

THE YOUNG BUNDY

Theodore Cowell came into the world in a home for unwed mothers. His own mother, 22-year-old Eleanor, had been sent there by her religious parents, who were humiliated by her pregnancy. Ted didn't know who his father was and, until much later in his life, he thought his mother was his sister. His grandparents brought him up as their adopted son, and he and his mother were often beaten by his grandfather. In 1951, Eleanor ran away, taking 5-year-old Ted with her. She married Johnnie Bundy, who adopted Ted as his son. Eleanor and Johnnie had several more children together.

Ted never liked his stepfather, and their relationship was strained; Ted thought Johnnie was uneducated, poor, and unworthy of his respect.

Throughout his childhood, Ted Bundy was a shy boy. He was intelligent and did well at school, but was bullied and didn't make friends easily. He graduated from the University of Washington with a degree in psychology in 1972. During this time, he had several girlfriends, but was heartbroken when Diane Edwards, a young woman who possessed wealth and status, broke up with him. This may have been a trigger for his later dark descent into murder; many of his victims resembled her.

"I DON'T FEEL GUILTY FOR ANYTHING. *I feel sorry for people who feel guilt.*"
—TED BUNDY

METHODS AND MOTIVES

It's thought that Bundy's terrifying and gruesome killing spree started around 1974, although Bundy himself hinted that he may have begun killing during his teens. His psychopathic nature had started to emerge back then; he was fascinated with knives, enjoyed mutilating small animals, and had voyeuristic tendencies.

On January 4, 1974, Bundy brutally attacked Karen Sparks in her Seattle apartment. Miraculously, Sparks survived, but was left with permanent disabilities. Shortly afterward, Lynda Healy became Bundy's first known murder victim. He broke into her apartment, knocked her unconscious, and carried her out to his car. Years later, part of her skull was found at one of his favored body dump sites.

Over the next year, Bundy targeted many women, mostly students. Wearing an arm sling or cast, he would lure them to his car on the pretence of needing help. Then, in what would become his signature modus operandi (M.O.), he would bludgeon them unconscious, then bind, rape, and torture them before killing, mutilating, and dumping them in remote wooded areas. He would often revisit the same sites to have sex with their corpses.

TIMELINE OF BUNDY'S MURDERS

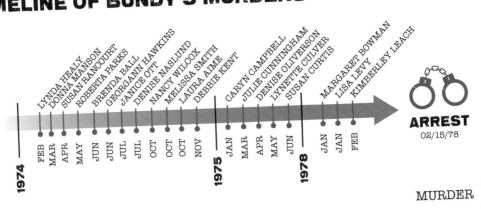

1974

LYNDA HEALY — FEB
DONNA MANSON — MAR
SUSAN RANCOURT — APR
ROBERTA PARKS — MAY
BRENDA BALL — JUN
GEORGANN HAWKINS — JUN
JANICE OTT — JUL
DENISE NASLUND — JUL
NANCY WILCOX — OCT
MELISSA SMITH — OCT
LAURA AIME — OCT
DEBBIE KENT — NOV

1975

CARYN CAMPBELL — JAN
JULIE CUNNINGHAM — MAR
DENISE OLIVERSON — APR
LYNETTE CULVER — MAY
SUSAN CURTIS — JUN

1978

MARGARET BOWMAN — JAN
LISA LEVY — JAN
KIMBERLEY LEACH — FEB

ARREST
02/15/78

MURDER

A national manhunt began for the unknown killer when bodies began to be discovered. Many young women remembered being approached by a man with his arm in a sling who tried to lure them into his brown VW Beetle. After a description was released to the public, Bundy was identified by four people—an ex-girlfriend, a colleague, a friend, and an old teacher of his. However, the police dismissed him as a suspect because he didn't fit their profile of the killer.

In August 1975, Bundy was pulled over by the police in Salt Lake City, and his car searched. They found ropes, tools, a crowbar, a mask, and handcuffs. This wasn't enough to arrest him, but he was put under surveillance. Later that month, Bundy kidnapped Carol DaRonch. She managed to escape and was able to identify him in a line-up. He was convicted of kidnap and assault, and received a 15-year sentence.

In 1977, Bundy managed to escape prison twice. He was caught eight days after his first attempt but was successful on his second try and he fled to Florida. Unable to resist his dark nature, Bundy started killing again. On January 14, 1978, he attacked four young female students and killed two of them: Margaret Bowman and Lisa Levy. He then broke into the apartment of Cheryl Thomas, who lived several blocks away, and beat her so badly that she permanently lost her hearing.

On February 9, 1978, he kidnapped and murdered 12-year-old Kimberly Diane Leach. This was to be the end of his murderous rampage. Days later, he was pulled over and arrested when the IDs of three dead women were found in his car. These, along with bite marks found on one of his victims, linked him to his last killings.

In 1979, Bundy was given two death sentences for the first-degree murders of Margaret Bowman and Lisa Levy, and was sentenced again in 1980 for the rape and murder of Kimberly Leach, for which he received a third death penalty.

DEATH

Bundy spent nine years appealing his sentence to no avail. Eventually, he confessed to 36 murders. On January 24, 1989, Ted Bundy, arguably one of 20th-century-America's most infamous and notorious serial killers, was executed by electric chair at the Florida State Prison in Raiford. Scientists examined his brain to see if they could find any physical abnormalities that could explain his cruel and violent behavior. The results were inconclusive.

POLICE
MIL WIS
227501
1-23-91

JEFFREY DAHMER

957 YEARS · 957 YEARS · 957 YEARS · 957 YEARS · 957 YEARS · 957 YEARS

THE YOUNG DAHMER

With his father often absent due to work and his mother frequently ill and addicted to prescription drugs, it was suggested by psychologists that Jeffrey Dahmer felt a sense of abandonment during his childhood. Chillingly, he developed a fascination with dead animals and roadkill, often probing his father, who was a research chemist, about how he could preserve animal bones. He began drinking heavily in his teenage years, a habit that carried on throughout his adulthood. Dahmer admitted he was often (if not always) drunk when he committed his heinous crimes.

Back in 1978, 18-year-old Jeffrey Dahmer was harboring a terrible secret.

He had just graduated from high school —and he also graduated from class clown to violent killer. He had lured a hitchhiking teenager, Steven Hicks, back to his father's house to listen to music and drink beer, but when Steven asked to leave, a switch flicked in Dahmer's brain. He didn't want the afternoon to end, so he pummeled Steven to death with a dumbbell.

This was the first of 17 tragic murders at the hands of a man whose motivation was a compulsive desire for power and control. Over the next four years, Dahmer's killing spree snowballed. He drugged, sexually assaulted, dismembered, photographed, preserved, and often cannibalized his victims.

"For what I did, I SHOULD BE DEAD."
—JEFFREY DAHMER

METHODS AND MOTIVES

The lines soon became blurred between Dahmer's childhood hobby of collecting animal bones and the preservation of the bones of his human victims.

Trying to preserve his victims became a case of trial and error; in his earlier murders, Dahmer boiled the skulls of his victims in a cocktail of industrial detergents and bleach in an attempt to save them. This made them too brittle and often resulted in Dahmer destroying them. However, he soon perfected his method of preservation using homemade solutions, acetone, spray-paint, or enamel. Dahmer's obsession with control and domination led him to try to create "zombie sex-slaves" of his victims. To do this, he drilled holes into their skulls and injected hydrochloric acid into their frontal lobes in an attempt to subdue them, not kill them. Yet in each of these cases, the injections ended their lives.

This might seem depraved enough, but Dahmer even went on to eat his victims' body parts. He admitted that he did this to feel closer to them, even after their deaths.

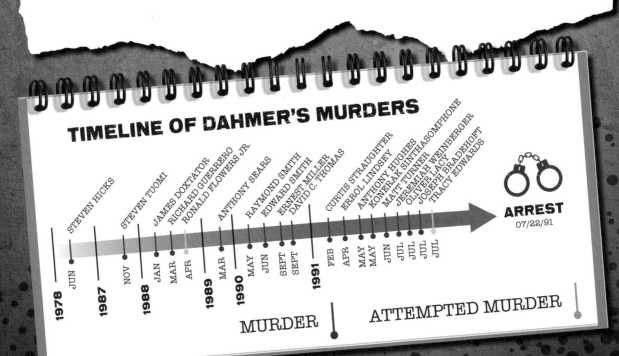

TIMELINE OF DAHMER'S MURDERS

STEVEN HICKS — JUN 1978
STEVEN TUOMI — NOV 1987
JAMES DOXTATOR — JAN 1988
RICHARD GUERRERO — MAR.
RONALD FLOWERS JR. — APR.
ANTHONY SEARS — MAR. 1989
RAYMOND SMITH — MAY 1990
EDWARD SMITH — JUN
ERNEST MILLER — SEPT
DAVID C. THOMAS — SEPT
CURTIS STRAUGHTER — FEB 1991
ERROL LINDSEY — APR.
ANTHONY HUGHES — MAY
KONERAK SINTHASOMPHONE — MAY
MATT TURNER — JUN
JEREMIAH WEINBERGER — JUL
OLIVER LACY — JUL
JOSEPH BRADEHOFT — JUL
TRACY EDWARDS — JUL

ARREST
07/22/91

MURDER | ATTEMPTED MURDER |

20

CAPTURE AND TRIAL

Eventually, Dahmer's reign of terror over Milwaukee came to an end. His would-be 18th victim, a man by the name of Tracy Edwards, managed to escape his clutches and flag down a police car, bringing the officers right back to Dahmer's doorstep. If the smell of the decomposing victims in his apartment wasn't enough to arrest him, the Polaroid photos of their bodies really were the coup de grâce.

The media circus that erupted after his July 1991 arrest took hold around the globe. Dahmer was tried for 15 counts of murder, the details of which were heard over a two-week period. He was found guilty on all counts, receiving 15 life sentences, and was later extradited to Ohio to be tried for his first murder in 1978, of the ill-fated Steven Hicks. He was found guilty once more, but was never tried for the second murder he confessed to, as he did not remember the event itself and the body had been destroyed.

*"The **ONLY MOTIVE** that there ever was, was to **COMPLETELY CONTROL** a person—a person I found physically attractive—and **KEEP THEM WITH ME FOR AS LONG AS POSSIBLE**, even if it meant just keeping **A PART OF THEM**."*
—JEFFREY DAHMER

DEATH

Jeffrey Dahmer met his own grisly end on November 28, 1994, when he was murdered by a fellow inmate, Christopher Scarver. Scarver was repulsed by Dahmer's crimes and he released his rage on the serial killer when they were paired together to clean the prison gym. Ironically enough, Dahmer was killed by a metal bar from the gym equipment—the same way he murdered his first victim.

MICHEL FOURNIRET

2 LIFE SENTENCES · 2 LIFE SENTENCES · 2 LIFE SENTENCES · 2 LIFE SENTENCES · 2 LIFE SENTENCES

THE YOUNG FOURNIRET

Fourniret was a quiet child with an above-average IQ. He liked classical music, literature, and playing chess, and he spoke in complex, formal French. While little is known about his childhood, Fourniret claimed he was sexually abused by his mother, and he later became obsessed with the symbol of virginity.

In the early 1960s, Fourniret served in the French Army during the Algerian War of Independence. He had a variety of jobs on his return, but struggled to keep any of them for long.

Over the next two decades, Fourniret was convicted numerous times for sexual offenses against minors, and was eventually jailed in 1984 for multiple sexual assaults. It was while he was in prison that he met his third wife, Monique Olivier, through an advertisement in a Catholic magazine for a pen pal. Olivier, who had been in a series of abusive relationships, began regularly writing to Fourniret. She promised to help him "hunt virgins" when he was released, if he promised to kill her former husband. The seeds for this deadly duo were sown.

"I needed to **HUNT VIRGINS** *twice a year. When I knew that I was going hunting and that I would bring something back,* **I DUG THE HOLES IN ADVANCE, THREE METERS DEEP."**

—MICHEL FOURNIRET

METHODS AND MOTIVES

Olivier was waiting for Fourniret at the prison gates on his release in 1987. A few weeks later, their heinous, 16-year-long killing spree began in France and Belgium. Olivier approached their first victim, 17-year-old Isabelle Laville. Pretending she needed directions, Olivier lured Isabelle into her white van. A little while later, she stopped again to pick up a "hitchhiker," who was in fact Fourniret. He got into the van where he proceeded to drug, rape, and strangle Isabelle to death.

The couple carried out their barbaric crimes in the van or back at their home. Fourniret would instruct Olivier to check whether the girls were virgins, then he would rape and kill them. He would either strangle, stab, or shoot them, or inject air into their veins to trigger a heart attack. Sometimes, he would sexually assault their corpses afterward.

Fourniret later stated that he needed to kill young women at least twice a year. He said he had been traumatized to discover that his first wife was not a virgin like himself, and that his feelings of frustration and betrayal over this had led to his crimes. He even believed that some of his victims looked like an incarnation of the Virgin Mary.

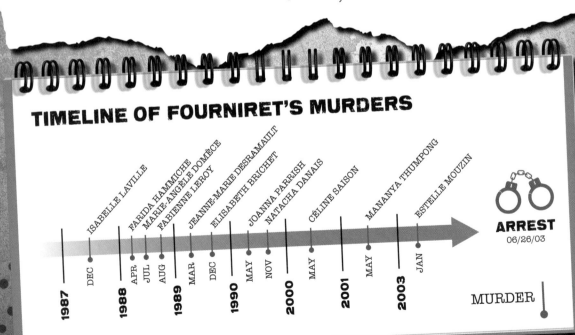

TIMELINE OF FOURNIRET'S MURDERS

- 1987
- ISABELLE LAVILLE — DEC
- 1988
- FARIDA HAMMICHE — APR
- MARIE-ANGÈLE DOMÈCE — JUL
- FABIENNE LEROY — AUG
- 1989
- JEANNE-MARIE DESRAMAULT — MAR
- ELISABETH BRICHET — DEC
- 1990
- JOANNA PARRISH — MAY
- NATACHA DANAIS — NOV
- 2000
- CÉLINE SAISON — MAY
- 2001
- MANANYA THUMPONG — MAY
- 2003
- ESTELLE MOUZIN — JAN

ARREST 06/26/03

MURDER

CAPTURE AND TRIAL

The failure to capture this evil pair highlighted serious faults in the French and Belgian legal systems, including limited sharing of criminal data. Fourniret had a criminal record, yet the police didn't connect him to any of the individual kidnappings and murders. In fact, the duo might have gotten away with it entirely, but in June 2003 the 13-year-old girl they had abducted bit through the ropes binding her wrists and jumped out of their van at some traffic lights. Fourniret and Olivier were then arrested.

Olivier confessed to some of their crimes, hoping that her sentence would be reduced. Fourniret, however, was uncooperative and unremorseful. During their trials in 2008, Fourniret only confessed to seven murders where the bodies had been found. He was sentenced to life without the possibility of parole. In 2018, he was given a second life sentence for the murder of Farida Hammiche, whom he had killed for money, which he then used to buy his château on the French-Belgian border. In 2018 he confessed to the murders of Joanna Parrish and Marie-Angèle Domèce, and in 2020, to the murder of Estelle Mouzin. He died before he could be tried for these last three murders.

Monique Olivier was found guilty in 2008 of being her husband's accomplice in at least five of the murders. She was sentenced to serve a minimum of 28 years of a life sentence for her complicity in Fourniret's crimes. In 2018, she was given a further 20 years for her part in Farida Hammiche's murder. In 2023, she was given another life sentence with a minimum term of 20 years for her complicity in the abductions of Joanna Parrish, Marie-Angèle Domèce and Estelle Mouzin. She admitted that her role in the crimes was "monstrous" and "unforgivable."

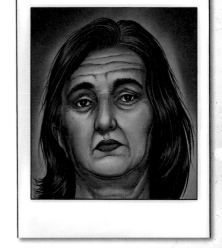

MONIQUE OLIVIER IS STILL INCARCERATED.

Michel Fourniret died on May 10, 2021, in a secure unit at La Pitié-Salpêtrière Hospital, where he had been admitted on April 28 from the nearby Fresnes prison. He was known to have had Alzheimer's disease and a heart condition.

POLICE DEPT.
DES PLAINES, ILL.
78-462 12-21-'78

JOHN WAYNE GACY

SENTENCED TO DEATH · SENTENCED TO DEATH · SENTENCED TO DEATH · SENTENCED TO DEATH

THE YOUNG GACY

John Wayne Gacy had a rough start in life. It was marred by abuse; his alcoholic father used to beat him and his sisters with a razor strap. Gacy was a sickly, overweight child with few friends, and he spent his teenage years in and out of the hospital due to a congenital heart condition. He struggled to come to terms with his homosexuality, and his father constantly belittled and humiliated him. He would spend the rest of his life searching for acceptance because his father made him feel like he was never good enough.

In 1968, Gacy was convicted for sexually assaulting a teenage boy.

He received a 10-year sentence but was released on parole in 1970. His first wife divorced him and took full custody of their two children. In 1971, he was again arrested for sexual assault, but the charges were dropped. With the help of his mother, Gacy bought a house in Cook County, Illinois, and became an independent building contractor. He became well-liked in his community, where he performed as a clown at charity events and children's parties, and he was active in civic and political groups, hoping one day to run as mayor and then for the state Senate. However, underneath this public front as a community man, Gacy held a dark secret: he had begun to kill.

"A CLOWN can get away with MURDER."
—JOHN WAYNE GACY

METHODS AND MOTIVES

Luring young men to his house with the promise of employment, Gacy would ply them with drugs or drinks, then handcuff, rape, and torture them. He would then kill his victims, usually by strangulation with a rope. He committed his first known murder in 1972 when he picked up 16-year-old Timothy McCoy at a bus stop and took him back to his house where he later stabbed him to death.

Over the following years up until his arrest in 1979, Gacy attacked and killed at least 33 young men. If he was known to have associated with one of his victims and questioned by the police, Gacy would say that the young man had told him he was planning on running away. Hiding behind his likable public persona, Gacy continued killing and getting away with his heinous crimes. 19-year-old Robert Donnelly, who Gacy raped and tortured, but allowed to leave his home on the condition that he told nobody what had happened to him, did report him to the police. Gacy said that Robert had agreed to consensual sex slavery, and the police believed him.

TIMELINE OF GACY'S MURDERS

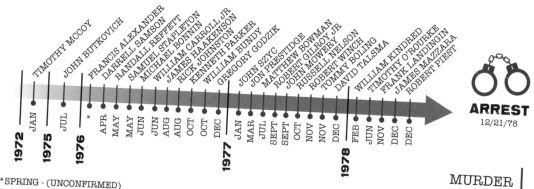

TIMOTHY MCCOY — 1972 JAN
JOHN BUTKOVICH — 1975 JUL
FRANCIS ALEXANDER — 1976 *
DARRELL SAMSON — APR
RANDALL REFFETT — MAY
SAMUEL STAPLETON — MAY
MICHAEL BONNIN — JUN
WILLIAM CARROLL — JUN
JAMES HAAKENSON — AUG
RICK JOHNSTON — AUG
KENNETH PARKER — OCT
WILLIAM BUNDY — OCT
GREGORY GODZIK — DEC
JOHN SZYC — 1977 JAN
JON PRESTIDGE — MAR
MATTHEW BOWMAN — JUL
ROBERT GILROY JR — SEPT
JOHN MOWERY JR — SEPT
RUSSELL NELSON — OCT
ROBERT WINCH — NOV
TOMMY BOLING — NOV
DAVID TALSMA — DEC
WILLIAM KINDRED — 1978 FEB
TIMOTHY O'ROURKE — JUN
FRANK LANDINGIN — NOV
JAMES MAZZARA — DEC
ROBERT PIEST — DEC

ARREST 12/21/78

* SPRING - (UNCONFIRMED)

MURDER

28

Finally, the police began to investigate Gacy after he was the last known person to have seen 15-year-old Robert Piest, who went missing on December 11, 1978. An initial search of Gacy's house revealed items belonging to some of his victims, as well as a gun, police badges, hypodermic needles, and pornography. Later, the police found the bodies of 29 young men on the property. Most were buried in the crawl space under his house, and some in the grounds nearby. A further four bodies were discovered in the Des Plaines River.

Gacy was arrested in late 1978, and convicted of 33 murders on March 12, 1980. He tried to plead that he was innocent by reason of insanity, as some psychologists had diagnosed him as schizophrenic. However, the jury dismissed this, and Gacy was sentenced to the death penalty and imprisoned in Menard Correctional Center in Chester, Illinois, for 14 years.

"That's when I realized that DEATH was the ULTIMATE THRILL."
—JOHN WAYNE GACY

DEATH

John Wayne Gacy was executed by lethal injection at Stateville Correctional Center in Crest Hill, Illinois, on May 10, 1994. Only 28 of the 33 bodies found have been conclusively identified. DNA investigations are ongoing to try to identify the remaining victims.

VERY IDHAM HENYANSYAH

SENTENCED TO DEATH · SENTENCED TO DEATH · SENTENCED TO DEATH · SENTENCED TO DEATH ·

THE YOUNG HENYANSYAH

Growing up, infidelity was a normal part of Henyansyah's life. His father had had an affair with his wife's sister and left the family home. Young Henyansyah was raised by his domineering mother, who had affairs with several men (including her own son-in-law) during his childhood. Controlled and treated harshly by his mother, Henyansyah felt isolated. He was conflicted by his homosexuality, which is considered sinful in parts of Indonesia.

When his mother sent him to a religious boarding school, Henyansyah immersed himself in his studies. It was here that he had a relationship with a male teacher. When this teacher later married a woman, Henyansyah felt betrayed. This may have been the trigger for what was to come. Already showing signs of narcissism and displaying an uncontrollable temper, 29-year-old Henyansyah began his horrific killing spree, murdering 11 people between 2006 and 2008.

"His acts were sadistic and inhuman, and caused deep sadness to the victims' families and anxiety in the community."
—JUDGE

METHODS AND MOTIVES

Henyansyah was motivated by his conflicting feelings about his own sexuality. His first victim was 27-year-old Guruh Setyo Pramono, with whom he had started a clandestine relationship after the relationship with his teacher ended. He then discovered that Pramono was seeing another man, and his innate jealous nature took over. Waiting until his mother was out, Henyansyah invited the unsuspecting Pramono back to his family home. There, during a frenzied attack, he stabbed and bludgeoned him to death with a crowbar. He then dismembered his body and dumped it in the fishpond behind his house. This would become his sadistic M.O.; 10 out of his 11 victims were buried in the fishpond.

His first five victims were boyfriends who cheated on him. He then killed his friend Nanik Hidayati and her 3-year-old daughter, Sylvia (who had witnessed her mother's brutal murder), when he discovered Hidayati had feelings for him. After this, he killed three male friends who were becoming suspicious of his behavior.

TIMELINE OF HENYANSYAH'S MURDERS

SPECIFIC DATES ARE UNKNOWN

GURUH SETYO PRAMONO
AGUSTINUS FITRI SETIAWAN
MUHAMMAD ACHSONI
ZAINUL ABIDIN
GRADY GLAND ADAM
NANIK HIDAYATI
SYLVIA RAMADANI PUTRI
MUHAMMAD ASRORI
VINCENTIUS YUDHY PRIYONO
ARIL SOMBA
HERI SANTOSO

ARREST
07/15/08

2006

2008

MURDER

CAPTURE AND TRIAL

Henyansyah decided to move to Jakarta in 2008, partly to cover his murderous tracks in his hometown. There, he mixed with the city's rich, gay community, offering sexual services in return for lavish gifts. He began a relationship with a man named Noval Andreas. When an old acquaintance, Heri Santoso, started showing an interest in Andreas, Henyansyah was furious. He lured Santoso to his apartment, where he savagely killed him, then placed his dismembered body in a suitcase which he left on the side of a road.

Henyansyah told Andreas what he had done. Although disgusted, Andreas didn't go to the police. Instead, the two men went on a spending spree using Santoso's credit card. This was to be Henyansyah's undoing. He was caught on CCTV using the credit card, and when the police went to his apartment, they discovered some of Santoso's belongings. Andreas confessed everything and was given a five-month sentence for his part in covering up the murder.

The investigation into Henyansyah's crimes uncovered the 10 bodies in the family fishpond. On April 6, 2009, he was tried and sentenced to death. He is currently awaiting execution at Kesambi Penitentiary in Cirebon, Java.

"Everyone has to die, and I'm ready."
—VERY IDHAM HENYANSYAH

Henyansyah is known as the "Singing Serial Killer" due to his antics behind bars. During his trial and sentencing, he entertained court officers, fellow inmates, and media audiences from his jail cell by singing songs from his (at the time) upcoming album.

FRITZ HAARMANN

SENTENCED TO DEATH · SENTENCED TO DEATH · SENTENCED TO DEATH · SENTENCED TO DEATH ·

THE YOUNG HAARMANN

Haarmann was the youngest of six children. His father was strict and distant, while his mother doted on him. As a young boy, Haarmann loved playing with dolls and wearing dresses. His father did not approve of this and, when Haarmann was 16, he sent him off to a military school to "toughen" him up. While there, Haarmann discovered that he had epilepsy. He was soon dismissed from the school and went to work in his father's cigar factory. It wasn't long before he committed his first crimes: sexually molesting young boys.

At that time, homosexuality was illegal in Germany and his behavior was seen as part of a mental illness. Haarmann was sent to a mental asylum, but he escaped and fled to Switzerland until 1900, when he returned to Germany to complete compulsory military service. In 1901, Haarmann was hospitalized due to his epilepsy and dismissed from the army a year later. His father tried many times, unsuccessfully, to have him put back in the asylum. Haarmann supplemented his small disability allowance with a string of petty crimes. In 1913, he was jailed for five years for burglary. He sat out World War I in his prison cell.

Released on parole in 1918, Haarmann moved into an apartment with his lover, Hans Grans, whom he had met in prison. He became a police informant while also working with a gang of smugglers.

"Believe me, I'm not ill—it's only that I occasionally have funny turns."
—FRITZ HAARMANN

METHODS AND MOTIVES

When young boys started disappearing in 1918, Haarmann came under suspicion, but the police didn't pursue their inquiries because he was a valuable informant. When he was later arrested for indecency with a minor, police failed to discover the severed head of one of his first known victims, Friedel Rohe, hidden behind his stove.

Conditions in post-war Germany were hard and Haarmann used this to his advantage, scouting for runaway teenage boys and coaxing them to his home with the promise of food and warmth. There, he would feed his victims, then bite them on their necks through their windpipes to kill them before sexually molesting their dead bodies. Then he would dismember them and it is rumored he ground their flesh into sausage meat which he may have later sold as beef or pork. He dumped any remains in the nearby River Leine, and he and Grans would sell the boys' clothes.

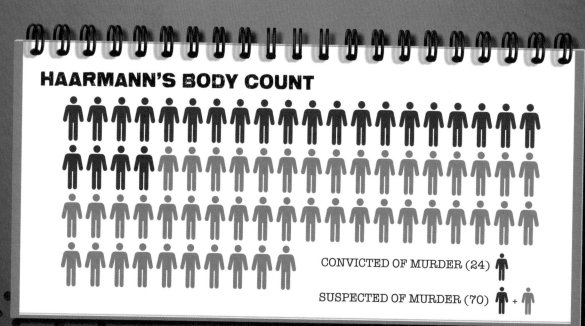

HAARMANN'S BODY COUNT

CONVICTED OF MURDER (24)

SUSPECTED OF MURDER (70)

For six years, Hanover police turned a blind eye to Haarmann's possible connection to the missing boys. It is thought he killed over 50 during this time. Then, in May 1924, skulls and skeletons were found on the banks of the River Leine. When the river was dragged, the bodies of over 20 victims were found.

An investigation was launched, and attention finally turned to Haarmann. When the police searched his apartment, they found the walls and floors stained with blood, and items of clothing from many of the boys. Only 27 of his victims have ever been identified.

Haarmann was arrested and a trial date was set. He was charged with 24 counts of murder and was sentenced to death. Hans Grans was sentenced to life in prison for his complicity in the gruesome murders, but his sentence was later commuted to just 12 years, and in 1975, he died a free man.

"I repent, but I do not fear death."
– FRITZ HAARMANN

On April 15, 1925, Haarmann was executed via decapitation by guillotine. The remains of his victims, found in the River Leine, were buried in a mass grave in Stöckener Cemetery that same year. Haarmann's head, which had been preserved in formaldehyde and given to the medical school in Göttingen, was only cremated in 2015.

Sadly, a terrible legacy of Haarmann's crimes was a wave of homophobia which swept through Germany, which the Nazis later capitalized on in their campaign to murder homosexuals.

JAVED IQBAL

SENTENCED TO DEATH · SENTENCED TO DEATH · SENTENCED TO DEATH · SENTENCED TO DEATH ·

THE YOUNG IQBAL

Javed Iqbal, one of eight children, grew up in a wealthy family in Lahore, Pakistan. His father was a respected and powerful businessman in the city. Little is known about Iqbal's childhood, but he was not known to have suffered any hardships. In fact, he was able to live a lavish lifestyle; his father bought him his own home and helped him start his own steel-casting business in 1978.

In 1985 and 1990, complaints of sodomy were filed against Iqbal, but he wasn't convicted and his father used his influence to keep his son out of prison. When his father died in 1993, Iqbal inherited more than ₹3,000,000 (Indian rupee) from him (around £28,000). He bought a bigger home and several cars, and set up various businesses such as a video store, a gym, and a small school. To the public, Iqbal seemed like a successful business and community man. In truth, he was a monster, using his businesses as a way to meet young men, whom he would groom and then sexually assault. Eventually, assault couldn't satisfy him, and the predator soon became a murderer.

*"I am Javed Iqbal, **KILLER OF 100 CHILDREN. I HATE** this world. I am **NOT ASHAMED** of my actions and I am **READY TO DIE. I have NO REGRETS. I KILLED 100 CHILDREN.**"*
—JAVED IQBAL

METHODS AND MOTIVES

In 1998, Iqbal and one of his young employees, Arbab, were badly beaten up and hospitalized. While they were recovering, Arbab's family filed a complaint against Iqbal. When he left the hospital, Iqbal was arrested and charged with sodomy. The charges were later dropped, but Iqbal, now penniless and homeless (due to local authorities selling his home and businesses to pay for his medical care), had to rent a house in a Lahore slum. This house would become the location of his horrific murders.

Between May and October 1999, Iqbal went on a frenzied killing spree. He lured young boys, mostly runaways or orphans living rough on the streets, to his home where he sexually assaulted them, strangled them to death with a chain, and then dismembered and disposed of their bodies in a vat of hydrochloric acid.

After his capture, Iqbal claimed that he had killed the boys as an act of revenge against the police, who he said had assaulted him and treated him unfairly after his arrest in 1998. He wanted to make 100 mothers experience the same pain and suffering his own mother had had to endure, watching her son's suffering, humiliation, and decline.

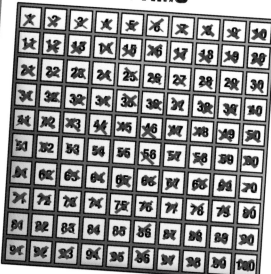

IQBAL'S VICTIMS

He kept **DETAILED RECORDS** of all his **VICTIMS,** *including their names, ages, and* **PHOTOGRAPHS.**

CAPTURE AND TRIAL

In November 1999, Iqbal sent a letter to the police and a local newspaper confessing to killing 100 boys. When the police raided his house, they were met with a gruesome scene: bloodstains on the walls and floors, bones, children's clothes and shoes, a chain, plastic bags containing handwritten notes and photos of his victims, and two vats with partially dissolved remains in them. They also found a note which claimed that Iqbal planned to drown himself in the Ravi River. When his body wasn't found, a huge manhunt was launched. On December 30, 1999, Iqbal turned himself in.

Iqbal was charged with 100 first-degree murders and given 100 death sentences on March 16, 2000. He later denied his guilt, saying that his confession had been made under duress, and was a hoax to bring attention to the plight of runaway children from poor families and the country's lack of concern for the poor.

The judge initially ruled that Iqbal be executed in the same brutal way he had killed his victims, and that under Sharia law, this should be done in public in front of the parents of the victims. However, human rights' laws wouldn't permit him to be executed in this manner.

*"He should be **STRANGLED 100 TIMES** with the chain he had used and **CUT UP INTO 100 PIECES** and **DISSOLVED IN ACID**, and [that] under Sharia law, this [should] **BE DONE IN PUBLIC** in front of **THE PARENTS OF THE VICTIMS.**"*

—JUDGE

DEATH

On October 9, 2001, Javed Iqbal was found dead in his cell at the Kot Lakhpat Jail, where he was being detained until his execution. His body was beaten, but despite all of the indications of foul play, his death was officially ruled as a suicide.

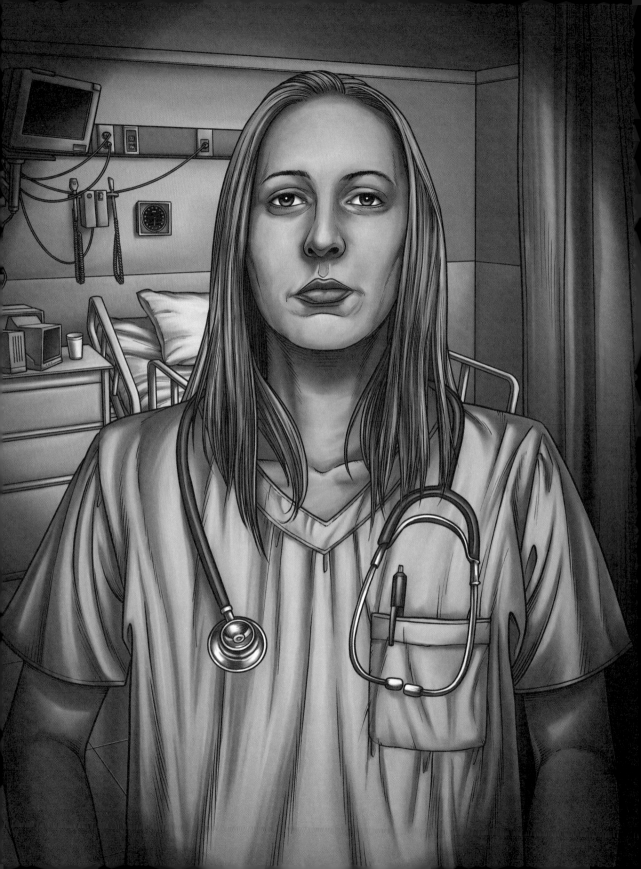

LUCY LETBY

15 LIFE SENTENCES · 15 LIFE SENTENCES · 15 LIFE SENTENCES · 15 LIFE SENTENCES ·

THE YOUNG LETBY

Letby was a quiet and unassuming only child. By all accounts, she had a happy childhood and adolescence in a loving family, where she was indulged and doted upon. She worked hard at school and college, and had a circle of good friends. After school, Letby went on to train as a nurse. In 2012, she started her first job on the neonatal unit at the Countess of Chester Hospital in Cheshire, England, where she worked until her arrest in 2018.

So, how did this outwardly caring young woman become one of the most prolific child murderers in modern British history, killing 7 babies and attempting to kill 7 more? How did she hide her dark, sadistic nature from her relatives, friends, and colleagues? And how was she able to carry out her heinous crimes in plain sight for so long, even after suspicions were raised?

"Sometimes I think, how do such sick babies get through and others just die so suddenly and unexpectedly? Guess it's how it's meant to be."

—LUCY LETBY (TEXT MESSAGE USED AS EVIDENCE)

METHODS AND MOTIVES

During 2015 and 2016, staff started to notice that the number of babies dying on the neonatal unit at the Countess of Chester Hospital was statistically higher than the normal number of expected deaths, especially since they were dying of serious catastrophic collapses that were not medically explicable.

On several occasions, valid staff concerns were dismissed. But as the number of babies dying or nearly dying increased, colleagues began to suspect something was very wrong. They noticed changes in Letby's behavior. She hovered around the grieving families, overly seeking their attention, and appearing to want to be seen as heroic for trying to save their babies, while attempting to garner sympathy and admiration from her colleagues. Outwardly, she played the role of the concerned nurse. In truth, she was a calculating opportunist who was murdering the babies in cold blood, either by injecting air or insulin into their bloodstreams or stomachs, or by physically abusing them or overfeeding them.

When the horrific details of her crimes were revealed, many psychologists diagnosed Letby as having a narcissistic personality disorder, possibly Munchausen's syndrome by proxy. A person with this disorder intentionally causes or fabricates illnesses or injuries to others while posing as a loving caregiver. They seek attention while thriving on the power and control they have, lacking empathy or remorse, but can mimic normal emotional responses and social behaviors.

I KILLED them on purpose. I am EVIL, I DID THIS.*

I don't deserve to live... I am an awful person.*

CAPTURE AND TRIAL

Finally, in 2017, the police were alerted and an investigation was launched. Letby was arrested on two separate occasions in 2018 and 2019, before being taken into custody in November 2020 when she was charged.

Her trial began in October 2022. Over the course of 10 months, the grueling details of her terrible crimes were revealed. Notes in her diary, including the murdered babies initials, were shown as evidence and helped secure her conviction. On August 21, 2023, Letby was found guilty of murdering 7 babies and attempting to murder 6 others. She pleaded not guilty to all the charges but was given 14 whole-life prison terms, without the possibility of parole.

On July 5, 2024, Letby was handed her 15th life sentence for the attempted murder of another premature baby in February 2016.

Letby is currently serving time in HMP Bronzefield, an all-female prison in Surrey, England. She continues to deny her crimes and is seeking permission to appeal her murder convictions.

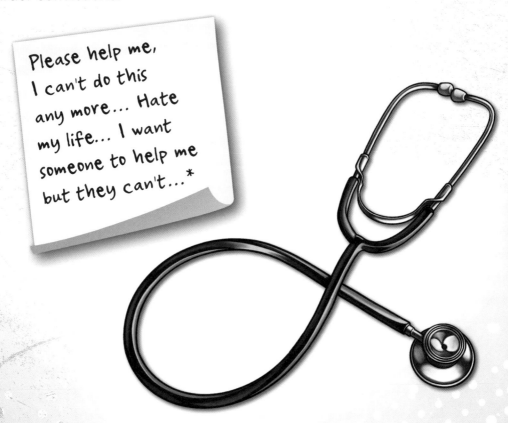

Please help me, I can't do this any more... Hate my life... I want someone to help me but they can't...*

*QUOTES FROM ACTUAL POST-IT NOTES FOUND IN LETBY'S HOME

COLLIER COUNTY
SHERIFF'S DEPT.
NAPLES, FLA.

33908 .0.6.2.4.93

SAMUEL LITTLE

CRIMINAL PROFILE:

Name: Samuel Little né McDowell

Date of birth: June 7, 1940

Place of birth: Reynolds, Georgia, USA

Also known as: The Choke-and-Stoke Killer

Victims: More than 60, probably 93

Convicted: Life sentence without the possibility of parole

LIFE WITHOUT PAROLE · LIFE WITHOUT PAROLE · LIFE WITHOUT PAROLE

THE YOUNG LITTLE

Samuel Little was born in Georgia, to a teenage mother who was a prostitute. She quickly abandoned him with his maternal grandmother, and he spent his childhood in Ohio. Little never knew his father. He struggled at school and eventually dropped out in his early teens. With no direction or discipline, the young Little turned to a life of petty crime. He was arrested for breaking and entering, and spent some time in juvenile detention.

From the mid-1950s, Little started traveling across America, criss-crossing states while committing crimes. By 1975, he had been arrested more than 25 times and had been in and out of prison, serving a total of around 10 years for everything from theft, fraud, DUIs, and assault to armed robbery, solicitation, and rape.

By 1982, Little had been arrested and acquitted of murder twice, in Florida and Mississippi.

"I say, if I can help get somebody **OUT OF JAIL,** *you know, then* **GOD MIGHT SMILE** *a little bit more on me."*

—SAMUEL LITTLE (CONFESSING TO MURDERS THAT OTHER PEOPLE HAD BEEN WRONGLY IMPRISONED FOR)

METHODS AND MOTIVES

Little claimed he killed 93 people across 19 states between 1970 and 2012. Since the FBI has confirmed that he committed at least 60 of these murders, Little has been named as the most prolific serial killer in American history. His confessions to the other 33 victims were deemed credible, but to date, law enforcement authorities do not have enough evidence to link them to Little with certainty.

He was able to get away with his heinous crimes for so long because he targeted people on the fringe of society. They were easy prey and not often missed until their bodies turned up. Most of his victims were women (usually women of color), and many of them were homeless, sex workers, or drug addicts.

Little would brutally rape and beat them until they were unconscious. He would then strangle them before dumping their bodies in secluded or wooded areas.

When he was later questioned as to his motives for killing so many people, he said that God had given him a mission to end their miserable lives. Sometimes he admitted he felt that he was possessed by the devil. Murder had become a thrill to him: "It was like drugs. I came to like it."

LITTLE'S PORTRAITS OF HIS VICTIMS

CAPTURE AND TRIAL

Eventually, Little's four-decade reign of terror came to an end. On September 5, 2012, he was arrested on a drug charge while he was living in a homeless shelter in Louisville, Kentucky. When his DNA linked him to three unsolved murders in California from the 1980s, Little was extradited to Los Angeles.

On January 7, 2013, Little was charged with these murders, and on September 25, 2014, he was found guilty on all three counts of first-degree murder and convicted. He was sentenced to life in prison without the possibility of parole.

Over the following years, Little confessed to more and more of his murders, giving detailed descriptions of his victims, where he killed them and what car he was driving at the time. He also painted pictures of many of the women he had murdered. The police were able to use some of these paintings to identify some of his victims.

In August 2019, he received a further two consecutive terms of life in prison and two consecutive sentences of 15 years to life on top of his prior sentences. At least 60 of his murders had been confirmed at this point.

"*I never killed* **NO SENATORS OR GOVERNORS OR FANCY NEW YORK JOURNALISTS.** *Nothing like that.* **I STAYED IN THE GHETTOS.**"
—SAMUEL LITTLE

DEATH

On December 30, 2020, Samuel Little died in custody in a Los Angeles hospital. Sadly, many of his victims have not been found, and many remain unidentified.

ALEXANDER PICHUSHKIN

THE YOUNG PICHUSHKIN

Pichushkin never knew his father, whom had walked out on the family when he was very young. Until the age of four, when he suffered a serious head injury, neighbors described Pichushkin as a polite and pleasant young boy who loved animals. After the accident, his personality changed; he became impulsive and was frequently hostile. He was bullied at school, so his mother sent him to a special school for children with learning difficulties, which he hated and found traumatic.

When Pichushkin left school, he moved in with his grandfather, whom he was very close to. He learned how to play chess, often playing the game in the park with other older men. Chess became a way for Pichushkin to channel his angry, aggressive feelings. It was also to become the macabre symbol of his murders. After his arrest, police found a notebook with a chessboard drawn in it and dates on 61 of the 64 squares. Pichushkin told them he had been trying to kill as many people as there were squares on the chessboard.

*"I was prosecutor, judge, and **EXECUTIONER.** I DECIDED who was to **LIVE** and who was to **DIE.**"*
—ALEXANDER PICHUSHKIN

METHODS AND MOTIVES

When Pichushkin's grandfather died, he became depressed. This may have triggered his killing spree, because he was angry that his grandfather had abandoned him. He got a dog as a companion, and would often walk it in Moscow's Bittsevsky Park, which would later become the killing ground for most of his murders.

In 1992, Pichushkin invited his friend, Mikhail Odiychuk, to go on a killing expedition with him. When Pichushkin realized Odiychuk was not prepared to kill anyone, he killed him instead.

It would be another 10 years before it was confirmed that Pichushkin killed again, although it is not known for certain whether he murdered anyone else during the 1990s.

There were a lot of homeless alcoholics and drug addicts around Bittsevsky Park. Pichushkin targeted them because they were easy prey and not easily missed. In what was to become his M.O., Pichushkin lured his victims into the park by asking them to come and have a drink with him at his dog's grave. He would then bludgeon them with a blunt instrument and throw their bodies into a sewage drain to hide them.

PICHUSHKIN'S BODY COUNT

CONVICTED MURDERS (48)

SUSPECTED TOTAL MURDERS (60)

CAPTURE AND TRIAL

In June 2006, Pichushkin invited Marina Moskalyova out for a walk. She was a colleague from the supermarket where he worked. Moskalyova left a note at home for her son, with Pichushkin's name and telephone number on it. When she didn't return home, her son contacted the police. Later, when her body was discovered, investigators found a metro ticket in her pocket. They reviewed CCTV footage from the station and saw her with Pichushkin.

Pichushkin was arrested for the murder of Moskalyova and convicted in October 2007 of killing 48 people and for attempting to kill a further 3. He said he had killed more people, but there was not enough evidence to convict him of these confessed crimes. His trial was aired on Russian TV. He was unrepentant and defiant in court, showing no remorse and believing his actions were "guided by the hand of God." He admitted that even if he had filled all the squares on his chessboard, he would have continued killing indefinitely, because he enjoyed it.

He was sentenced to life imprisonment and sent to a hard-labor colony called the Polar Owl. He also had to undergo psychiatric treatment for "a personality disorder expressed in a sadistic inclination to murder." Pichushkin is still serving out his sentence. He was not found to be mentally ill, although the damage he sustained to his frontal lobe as a child is linked to criminal violence, aggressive behavior, and psychopathy.

Pichushkin was not given the death sentence because Russia has maintained a moratorium on capital punishment since 1996, as part of its obligations to the Council of Europe.

MIKHAIL POPKOV

THE YOUNG POPKOV

Very little is known about Mikhail Popkov's childhood, other than it was unhappy. His mother was an alcoholic and allegedly abused him. This would lead to a lifetime of resentment toward women, particularly those who resembled her.

Popkov worked as a policeman and later, a security guard. His wife was also a police officer, and they had a daughter together. To the outside world, they looked like the perfect happy family. Little did anyone know that Popkov, a loving husband, father, and upstanding member of the community, was a sadistic killer, who murdered and butchered at least 86 women (likely closer to 200) between 1992 and 2012.

When the Soviet Union collapsed in 1991, Angarsk, the city in the remote Siberian Irkutsk region where Popkov lived and worked, became rife with criminal activity. There was so much violence that many murders were not investigated. So, when mutilated bodies started showing up in the forest around the city in the mid-1990s, the police attributed it to criminal gangs. This gave Popkov the perfect cover for his crimes.

"COMMITTING the MURDERS, I was GUIDED by MY INNER CONVICTIONS."
—MIKHAIL POPKOV

METHODS AND MOTIVES

Motivated by his hatred toward women who reminded him of his abusive, alcoholic mother, Popkov saw it as his mission to "cleanse the streets" of women who engaged in behavior he considered immoral. He would cruise the streets of Angarsk (or other towns in the region), looking for prostitutes or vulnerable drunk women leaving bars alone. Using his uniform and police car to gain the trust of his victims, he would offer them a ride home. Once they were in his car he would drive out to the forest, where he would rape, torture, butcher, and mutilate them with knives, axes, screwdrivers, spades, ropes, or baseball bats, before killing them. He would then rape their lifeless bodies once again.

Even though Popkov was identified in 1998 by one of only three young women who survived his brutal attacks, the police didn't follow up with an investigation because his wife gave him an alibi. Popkov continued killing until his arrest in 2012. He even helped the police work the crime scenes of some of his own murders.

POPKOV'S CRIME COUNT

ARREST
06/23/12

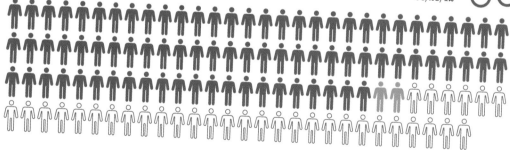

CONVICTED MURDERS (82)   ATTEMPTED MURDERS (2)   CONFESSED MURDERS (116+)

CAPTURE AND TRIAL

On June 23, 2012, Popkov was finally detained under the suspicion of raping and killing three women earlier that year. He confessed to dozens more murders, and his DNA was matched to a rape from 2003. He said he had only stopped because he had become impotent.

In October 2012, Popkov was charged with 22 murders and 2 attempted murders. His case went to trial in May 2014, and on January 14, 2015, he was sentenced to life imprisonment in Black Dolphin, a high-security prison on the remote Russian border with Kazakhstan, which holds Russia's most brutal and dangerous criminals. He was spared execution by firing squad because of Russia's moratorium on the death penalty.

In March 2017, Popkov confessed to and was charged for another 60 offenses. Since then, he confesses to more murders every year, bringing the total number of his heinous crimes closer to 200 so far.

Under a scheme adopted by the Russian Army, any prisoner who fights in the continuing Ukraine war and survives for six months can be pardoned. Popkov applied for the scheme, but his request was denied. He is still serving his sentence.

DENNIS RADER

175 YEARS WITHOUT PAROLE · 175 YEARS WITHOUT PAROLE · 175 YEARS WITHOUT PAROLE · 175 YEARS WITHOUT PAROLE

THE YOUNG RADER

Dennis Rader was the oldest of four sons, and he enjoyed a seemingly normal childhood. Although he was a withdrawn, introverted child, he joined the Boy Scouts and was an active member of the Lutheran church that his family belonged to. His father was in the US Marine Corps, so was away from home a lot.

Behind this quiet, unassuming façade, however, Rader masked his true dark nature. As a teenager, he would secretly hang and strangle cats and dogs in his neighborhood, and he fantasized about tying girls up and having sex with them.

In the mid-1960s, Rader dropped out of college and joined the US Air Force. During this time, he would peep through windows in his neighborhood to watch women undress and often broke into their homes to steal their underwear.

In 1971, Rader got married. To the outside world he presented himself as an attentive and caring husband and father, a good employee, and a pillar of his community. His wife and two children didn't realize that they were living with a monster, who tortured and killed at least 10 victims between 1974 and 1991 in their Wichita, Kansas neighborhood.

"A DEMON *that's* WITHIN ME. *It kind of* CONTROLS ME."
—DENNIS RADER

METHODS AND MOTIVES

In 1973, Rader lost his job and became depressed. This was probably the trigger that turned his devious fantasies and obsession with pornography into something much worse. He began driving around his local area and school campuses, watching women and fantasizing about how he might kidnap them at gunpoint and strangle them with his bare hands.

On January 15, 1974, he broke into the home of one of his co-workers, Julie Otero. He strangled Julie, her husband, and son, and hanged her 11-year-old daughter in the basement. A few months later, he stabbed another co-worker, Kathryn Bright, to death in her home.

Giving himself the moniker "BTK" (bind, torture, kill), Rader established his horrific M.O. He tortured and killed to satisfy his sexual desires, leaving his BTK signature carved on his victims' bodies. He saw himself as a natural predator and killing as an accomplishment.

Unusually for a serial killer, Rader was able to "cool off" between murders, disappearing before he could be caught and living a "normal" life for years before killing again. Instead, using trophies from his victims, he would engage in autoerotic fantasies to relive each murder. When his urges became too strong, BTK would strike again.

TIMELINE OF RADER'S MURDERS

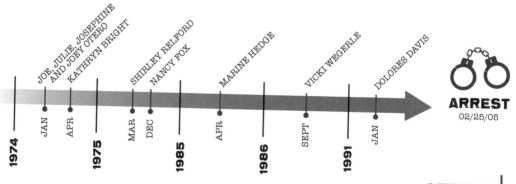

- JOE, JULIE, JOSEPHINE AND JOEY OTERO — JAN
- KATHRYN BRIGHT — APR
- SHIRLEY RELFORD — MAR
- NANCY FOX — DEC
- MARINE HEDGE — APR
- VICKI WEGERLE — SEPT
- DOLORES DAVIS — JAN

1974 1975 1985 1986 1991

ARREST 02/25/05

MURDER

CAPTURE AND TRIAL

Ultimately, it was Rader's narcissism that was his undoing. Craving public notoriety and wanting to be regarded like other serial killers, such as the Son of Sam and the Boston Strangler, Rader, still at large, began taunting the media, sending them messages, letters, and clues as to his identity. Starting in October 1974, Rader contacted a local newspaper after they published an article in which three men had confessed to murdering the Otero family, directing them to look inside a particular book at the local library. Inside the book was a letter:

"Those three dudes you have in custody are just talking to get publicity . . . The code words for me will be . . . Bind them, torture them, kill them, BTK, you see he's at it again. They will be on the next victim."

The taunts and clues continued over the years, with Rader becoming more careless the more attention he craved, leaving items of his victims to be found, word grid clues revealing his name and house number, Barbie dolls posed in death positions with hoods over their heads, a signatured cereal box, and photos from his crime scenes.

Finally, in February 2005, Rader was caught and taken into custody. He had sent a CD to the local TV station with more clues. Unknown to Rader, the police were able to identify him and his location from the hidden metadata on the disc.

Rader was unremorseful; his only regret was having been caught. At first he denied any of the charges, but later changed his plea and provided explicit details of his crimes. On August 18, 2005, Rader was charged with 10 counts of first-degree murder, and received a sentence of 10 consecutive life terms in prison, for a minimum of 175 years without the possibility of parole. He is currently serving out his sentence at El Dorado Correctional Facility. Because he committed his crimes before Kansas introduced the death penalty in 1994, this sentence wasn't applicable to him.

Police are still looking into other unsolved crimes that might be linked to BTK.

RICHARD RAMIREZ

SENTENCED TO DEATH • SENTENCED TO DEATH • SENTENCED TO DEATH • SENTENCED TO DEATH •

THE YOUNG RAMIREZ

Richard Ramirez was the youngest of five children born to Mexican immigrants. He was physically abused by his father and reportedly sustained multiple head injuries at an early age. This could have caused his epilepsy, which he developed around the age of five. Ramirez suffered from regular seizures well into his teens, which affected his schoolwork.

When Ramirez was 12 years old, an older cousin whom he looked up to showed him photos of women he had allegedly raped, tortured, and killed. The following year, Ramirez witnessed the same cousin shooting his wife dead.

This was a pivotal moment in the young Ramirez's life. He began sniffing glue and smoking marijuana, eventually becoming a heavy drug user. He also started breaking into other people's homes.

Ramirez dropped out of school in the ninth grade. Over the next decade, he fell into a life of petty crime and was arrested on several occasions for possession of drugs or theft. By the time he moved to Los Angeles at the age of 18, Ramirez was a cocaine addict, neglecting his personal hygiene (resulting in rotting teeth), and had developed a macabre interest in Satanism.

> *"Hey,* **BIG DEAL. DEATH** *always* **COMES WITH THE TERRITORY.** *I'll see you in* **DISNEYLAND."**
> – RICHARD RAMIREZ (HIS RESPONSE WHEN GIVEN HIS DEATH SENTENCE)

METHODS AND MOTIVES

Between 1984 and 1985, Ramirez committed around 30 violent crimes, raping and torturing his victims, and killing at least 13 people. He was likely motivated by a combination of his unhappy, abusive childhood, his traumatic head injuries, his prolonged drug abuse, and his Satanic beliefs.

During a burglary on June 28, 1984, Ramirez carried out his first known murder. He raped and stabbed 79-year-old widow Jennie Vincow to death, slashing her throat so deeply that he nearly decapitated her. Eight months later, during the spring and summer of 1985, Ramirez reignited his terrifying killing rampage.

Ramirez would break into a family home, shoot the husband, then rape and torture the wife before stabbing or bludgeoning her to death. If there were children present, he would sometimes molest them but spare their lives. He would leave Satanic symbols at the crime scenes, often carved into the bodies of his victims. Some of his victims survived the brutal assaults; they reported that he had forced them to profess their love for Satan to him.

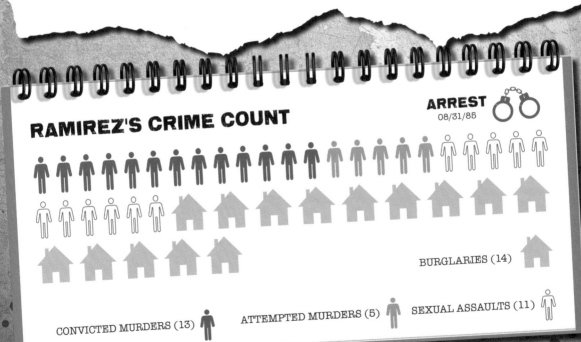

RAMIREZ'S CRIME COUNT

ARREST
08/31/85

BURGLARIES (14)

CONVICTED MURDERS (13)   ATTEMPTED MURDERS (5)   SEXUAL ASSAULTS (11)

CAPTURE AND TRIAL

Ramirez's last night of terror, on August 24, 1985, would lead to his eventual capture. His victim survived the attack, and was able to give the police a detailed description of Ramirez, his car, and his license plate number. His abandoned vehicle was found a few days later and fingerprints in it were matched to his criminal record. Ramirez's name and photo were released to the public.

On August 31, 1985, Ramirez was spotted by members of the public, who notified the police. A crowd of people surrounded him and beat him up until the police arrived.

Ramirez's trial began in early 1989. He showed no remorse throughout and made many references to Satan. On September 20, 1989, he was found guilty of 43 charges, convicted of 13 first-degree murders, 5 counts of attempted murder, 11 sexual assault charges, and 14 burglary charges.

When Ramirez was sentenced to death by gas chamber on November 7, 1989, he remained defiant and dismissive.

> *"SERIAL KILLERS do ON A SMALL SCALE what GOVERNMENTS do on a LARGE ONE. They are A PRODUCT OF THE TIMES, and these are BLOODTHIRSTY TIMES."*
> —RICHARD RAMIREZ

DEATH

Richard Ramirez was diagnosed with cancer while serving his sentence on death row at San Quentin State Prison, California. He died on June 7, 2013, before he could be executed.

Ramirez is believed to have committed other murders and crimes, but was never charged for them.

GARY RIDGWAY

48 LIFE SENTENCES + 480 YEARS · 48 LIFE SENTENCES + 480 YEARS · 48 LIFE SENTENCES + 480 YEARS

THE YOUNG RIDGWAY

The young Ridgway was raised in a deprived neighborhood near Seattle's Pacific Highway and SeaTac Airport. He was dyslexic and struggled at school, being an anxious child. He wet the bed well into his teenage years, and his mother washed him inappropriately after each occurrence, causing him to have conflicted emotions toward her.

By the 1960s, Ridgway was beginning to show signs of his dark and disturbed nature. At 16, he stabbed a young boy, but the boy survived and no charges were brought against him.

In 1969, he joined the US Navy and served two years. On his return to Seattle, Ridgway got a job as a truck painter. Over the next 30 years, he would marry three times, and he had one son with his second wife. During his second marriage, Ridgway became fanatical about religion. While publicly living a normal family and working life, Ridgway began his horrific killing spree, raping and murdering as many as 80 women and girls during the 1980s and 1990s. At the time of his sentence in 2003, Ridgway had committed more murders than any other serial killer in American history.

"I KILLED SO MANY WOMEN I have a hard time keeping them straight."
—GARY RIDGWAY

METHODS AND MOTIVES

It is believed Ridgway began his killing spree in 1982, shortly after he was arrested (but not charged) for solicitation. The body of 16-year-old Wendy Caulfield, who went missing after leaving her foster home, was found in the Green River on July 15, 1982. She had been raped and strangled. Over the course of the next month, seven more bodies were discovered in the river and surrounding area.

Ridgway, who had been harboring a lifetime of hatred toward his mother and had fantasized about killing her, channeled his rage and religious fervor against vulnerable runaway girls and prostitutes; easy targets who probably wouldn't be reported as missing as quickly as others. Later, after his capture, he claimed that he hated prostitutes and wanted to kill as many of them as possible.

Between 1982 and 1984, Ridgway brutally raped and killed more than 40 women. Many of his earlier victims were found in or near the Green River, and others were found in remote wooded areas around Washington's Pacific Highway. Ridgway would continue killing until 1998.

RIDGWAY'S BODY COUNT

ARREST
11/30/01

CONVICTED MURDERS (48)   SUSPECTED TOTAL MURDERS (80)

CAPTURE AND TRIAL

With the body count increasing, the police formed a task force in August 1982 to search for the "Green River Killer," as he had been dubbed. Ridgway, who had an existing criminal record, was a suspect several times over the course of the investigation. He was questioned and his house was searched, but no evidence could be found to link him to the crimes.

Eventually, on November 30, 2001, Ridgway was arrested. Forensic tests, which had become much more sophisticated, linked his DNA to four of the victims.

Ridgway confessed to the crimes, but showed no remorse. On November 5, 2003, he accepted a plea deal that spared him the death penalty, agreeing to reveal the location of more bodies which had not yet been discovered. On December 18, 2003, Ridgway was sentenced to 48 consecutive life sentences, without the possibility of parole, for aggravated first-degree murder, with an additional 480 years for tampering with evidence.

He is currently serving his sentence in Washington State Penitentiary in Walla Walla. Many of his victims have still not been identified and some still haven't been found.

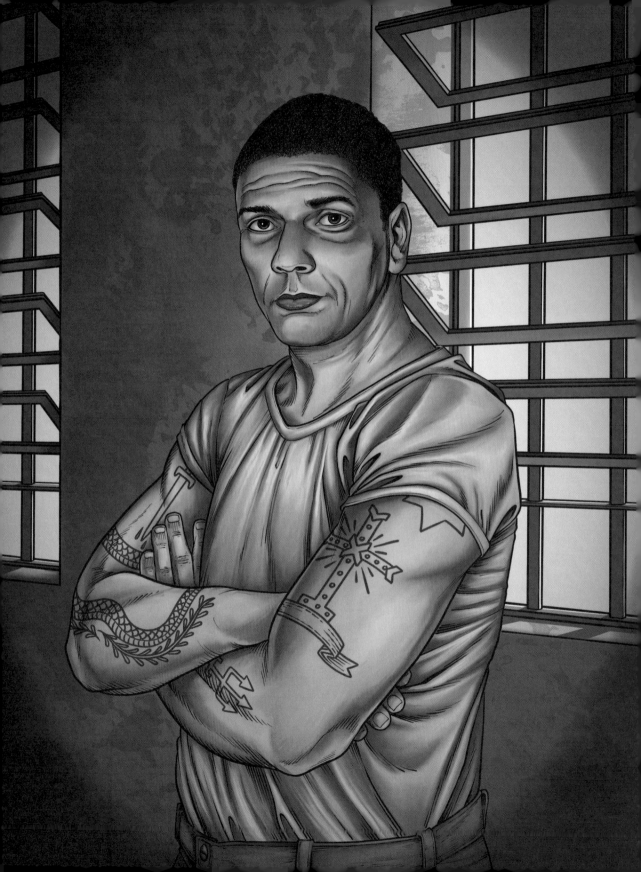

PEDRO RODRIGUES FILHO

400 YEARS · 128 YEARS · 400 YEARS · 128 YEARS · 400 YEARS · 128 YEARS

THE YOUNG RODRIGUES

Pedro Rodrigues Filho was born with an injured skull as a result of his father beating his mother during her pregnancy. His father physically abused both Rodrigues and his mother throughout Rodrigues' childhood, later killing his mother with a machete.

Rodrigues was only 14 years old when he first killed someone. He shot and killed the deputy mayor of his hometown because the man had fired his father, who was a school security guard, over accusations that he had stolen food from the school kitchen.

Later, Rodrigues shot the security guard whom he suspected had really stolen the food.

Rodrigues fled to São Paulo. There, he continued his killing spree, robbing drug dens and killing dealers. Still at large, he became known in the media as a vigilante called Pedrinho Matador.

It was in São Paulo that Rodrigues met and fell in love with a girl named Maria Aparecida Olympia. She was pregnant with his child when she was murdered by a local gang leader, who sought revenge on Rodrigues for the murders he had already carried out.

"I swore revenge in front of my mother's coffin . . ."
—PEDRO RODRIGUES FILHO

His partner's death pushed Rodrigues over the edge. He wanted revenge, so he tracked down the people directly responsible for her murder then tortured and killed them. He then went on to kill every remaining member of the gang, massacring them at a wedding organized by the gang leader.

The apple hadn't fallen very far from the tree—a childhood of abuse and violence had sowed the seeds for the dangerous and violent monster Rodrigues had become. Between 1968 and 2003, he murdered at least 71 people, 47 of whom were fellow prison inmates he killed while he was incarcerated. Rodrigues claimed that he never killed innocent people, despite sporting a tattoo that said, "I kill for pleasure" ("Mato por prazer"). His motive was anger and a desire for revenge; he saw himself as a vigilante and believed the people he killed deserved to die.

Rodrigues continued his vigilante killings, stabbing and hacking his victims to death, until he was first apprehended on May 24, 1973.

RODRIGUES' BODY COUNT

ARREST
05/24/73

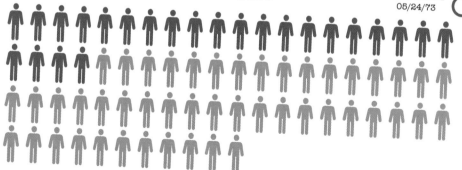

MURDERS BEFORE ARREST (24)   FELLOW INMATES (47)

On the way to prison in a police car, Rodrigues killed a rapist who was traveling in the car with him. At his trial, he was sentenced to 128 years in prison. However, Brazilian law at the time only allowed a maximum prison sentence of 30 years (it has since been increased to 40 years).

Behind bars, Rodrigues' murderous vendettas did not stop. Over the next 3 decades he killed 47 inmates, including his own father, who was in the same prison as him. Rodrigues had vowed to get revenge for his mother's murder; he stabbed his father 22 times, then ripped his heart out of his chest and bit into it.

Rodrigues was given an additional 400 years for the killings he committed in prison, but he only served an extra 4 years on top of his 30-year sentence and was released on April 24, 2007.

It was not long before he was back in prison again. In 2011 he was charged with illegal possession of weapons and for threatening others, but Rodrigues knew how to play the system, and in 2018, he was released early for good behavior.

Rodrigues launched his own YouTube channel after his release from prison, using his life as a cautionary tale to others and campaigning against violent crime. He is also said to have been the inspiration for *Darkly Dreaming Dexter*, a book by American novelist Jeff Linsey, which later was adapted to become the hit TV series, *Dexter*.

DEATH

On March 5, 2023, Rodrigues was killed outside a family member's home in São Paulo. He was shot and his throat was slashed. Although it is not known who killed him, it was likely a revenge killing for one of the many victims of the serial killer himself.

TAKAHIRO SHIRAISHI

SENTENCED TO DEATH • SENTENCED TO DEATH • SENTENCED TO DEATH • SENTENCED TO DEATH •

THE YOUNG SHIRAISHI

Not much is known about Takahiro Shiraishi's childhood. He was a quiet, diligent student on the baseball and track teams in elementary and high school. When he was a teenager, his parents divorced, and his mother and younger sister moved out of the family home. This may have been a trigger for his later monstrous crimes.

Shiraishi was close to his father, but after his mother left, his life turned down a darker path. School friends later recounted how they used to play choking games with Shiraishi, taking turns to choke each other until they passed out. They remember Shiraishi enjoying this game a little too much.

Around 2011, Shiraishi began working in one of Tokyo's red-light districts as a scout, luring young women to work in the sex parlors. It wasn't long before he was arrested and given a suspended sentence for illegally prostituting minors.

Struggling with his mental health, and unable to form a healthy relationship with a woman himself, Shiraishi developed an obsession with suicide. He set up several profiles on Twitter, with names like "Hangman," "Hanging Pro," and "I Want to Die," and it would be through these online accounts that he found and groomed his future victims.

*"I want to **HELP PEOPLE** who are really **IN PAIN.** Please **DM ME ANYTIME.**"*
—TAKAHIRO SHIRAISHI

METHODS AND MOTIVES

Between August and October 2017, Shiraishi carried out his macabre crimes, killing eight women and one man (the boyfriend of his first victim) to prevent him from telling anyone about his secrets.

Pretending to be suicidal himself, Shiraishi would initiate conversations with vulnerable women online, telling them he could help or watch them die. He would then arrange to meet them and take them back to his apartment. If the women were wealthy, he would manipulate them into giving him money, letting them leave if he thought he could continue to take money from them. If he saw no monetary value in them, he would drug them so they couldn't resist assault, then brutally rape them before strangling them to death. He then mutilated their bodies and stored them in coolers in his apartment.

Motivated by greed, his violent sexual fantasies, and his twisted need for love and attention, Shiraishi was a master of manipulation. He later confessed that if he hadn't been caught, he would have continued murdering indefinitely.

TIMELINE OF SHIRAISHI'S MURDERS

MIZUKI MIURA — 21ST
KUREHA ISHIHARA — 28TH
SHOGO NISHINAKA — 29TH
HINAKO SARASHINA — 15TH
HITOMI FUJIMA — 23RD
AKARI SUDA — 26TH
NATSUMI KUBO — 30TH
KAZUMI MARUYAMA — 18TH
AIKO TAMURA — 21ST

ARREST
10/31/17

AUG

SEPT

OCT

NOV

2017

MURDERS

CAPTURE AND TRIAL

Shiraishi's Twitter presence was to be his undoing. When the brother of his final victim tried to find out what had happened to his missing sister, he became suspicious of her messages with Shiraishi on Twitter. He alerted the police who set up a trap to find Shiraishi.

On October 31, 2017, Shiraishi went to meet a woman who had messaged him. The police were waiting. They followed the pair back to the apartment, where Shiraishi was arrested. The police found the disembodied remains and bones of his nine victims stored in coolers, along with the blood-soaked tools he had used to cut them up.

At his trial, Shiraishi tried to argue that his victims had given him their permission to be killed. He later confessed to the murders, and on December 15, 2020, he was sentenced to death by hanging. Shiraishi is currently in prison waiting for his execution.

The killings shocked Japan's citizens. Japan has one of the highest suicide rates in the world, and Shiraishi's cold and calculated use of social media to manipulate vulnerable people triggered a fresh debate about how to help those considering suicide, and how to stop social media being used as a tool to encourage it.

HAROLD SHIPMAN

CRIMINAL PROFILE:

Name: Harold Shipman

Date of birth: January 14, 1946

Place of birth: Bestwood, Nottingham, UK

Also known as: Doctor Death

Victims: Around 250

Convicted: Life sentence without the possibility of parole

THE YOUNG SHIPMAN

Harold Shipman grew up in an ordinary, working-class British family. There are no indications that he had an unhappy childhood. He was an intelligent young man, and he went on to study medicine at the University of Leeds. His mother died of lung cancer in 1963. Shipman was her favorite child; she had spoiled him and instilled in him a sense of superiority and arrogance. He was devastated by her death. Shipman became interested in medicine while he helped to care for her, and was particularly fascinated by the morphine drugs given to her to relieve her pain.

In 1966, Shipman married a woman named Primrose and they had four children together. He became a GP in 1970, but was dismissed from the practice in 1975 when it was discovered that he had been writing fraudulent prescriptions for meperidine, to which he had become addicted. He was convicted of forgery and had to go into drug rehabilitation. By 1977 he was practicing medicine again, and by 1993 he was able to set up his own practice. He had an established reputation and was renowned for his good bedside manner.

It was behind this façade of a normal family and working life that one of the most prolific serial killers in English history managed to hide his deadly crimes for almost 30 years.

*"The police complain **I'M BORING**. No mistresses, home abroad, money in Swiss banks, I'm normal. If that is boring, **I AM**."*
—HAROLD SHIPMAN

METHODS AND MOTIVES

Between 1971 and 1998, Shipman murdered around 250 of his patients. He killed his first known victim, 70-year-old Eva Lyons, in March 1975. Any unexplained deaths of his patients prior to 1975 were never proven to have been the result of murder.

Abusing his position of trust and responsibility as a doctor, Shipman targeted mostly vulnerable, elderly patients. In most cases, he would inject his victims with a lethal dose of the painkiller diamorphine, then he waited for them to die. If a relative was present, Shipman would pretend to call emergency services and then cancel the call when they died. He then signed their death certificates as death by natural causes, saying no autopsy was needed and often recommending that the patient be cremated rather than buried.

Shipman's motives were unclear. His mother's untimely death may have been a trigger, and he could have been seeking to avenge her death. The arrogant doctor certainly enjoyed having the power of life or death over his patients. It has been suggested that he saw himself as some sort of angel of mercy, killing the elderly who might go on to become a burden on the health care system.

SHIPMAN'S BODY COUNT

ARREST
09/07/98

MURDERED PATIENTS (250)

FIRST VICTIM – EVA LYONS, 70 (1975)

LAST VICTIM – KATHLEEN GRUNDY, 81 (1998)

CAPTURE AND TRIAL

Over the years, suspicions did fall on Shipman, but they were quickly dismissed because the paperwork seemed to be in order, and investigations were dropped. A local undertaker had questioned Shipman when he noticed that there was an unusually high number of elderly deaths in the community and that many of the patients had been found in similar death poses, fully clothed and usually reclining on a couch. Shipman had a criminal record from 1975, but not once was this looked into.

Finally, Shipman's killing spree came to an end. Angela Woodruff, the daughter of his last victim, Kathleen Grundy, did not believe the explanations given for her 81-year-old mother's sudden death on June 24, 1998. Kathleen had been in good health and then had died shortly after Shipman had visited her at home. Even more suspicious was the fact that Kathleen's will had been changed, bequeathing her whole estate to Shipman.

Woodruff had her mother's body exhumed and an autopsy revealed that she had died of a morphine overdose, administered within three hours of her death. Shipman's home was raided and medical records, jewelry, and an old typewriter used to forge the will were found, as well as false prescriptions and a stash of unused drugs that he had stolen from his patients. A full investigation was launched. The time stamps on Shipman's computer showed when and how he had altered the medical records of his victims, listing symptoms they didn't have to cover his tracks.

Shipman was arrested on September 7, 1998. He denied all charges, regularly changing his story. On January 31, 2000, he was found guilty of 15 counts of first-degree murder and 1 count of forgery. As a result, he was given 15 life sentences for the murders and 4 years for the forgery, which all commuted to a whole life sentence, without the possibility of parole.

DEATH

On January 13, 2004, Shipman hanged himself in his cell at HMP Wakefield, England.

PETER SUTCLIFFE

THE YOUNG SUTCLIFFE

Peter Sutcliffe grew up in a Catholic, working-class family with five younger siblings. As a teenager, Sutcliffe was a loner. The signs of the monster he was to become began to show themselves due to his voyeuristic tendencies. Sutcliffe wasn't a good student and he left school when he was just 15. He worked at several different jobs before getting a part-time job in a morgue and becoming a gravedigger.

He often bragged to his friends that he robbed the bodies that arrived at the morgue.

In the mid-1970s, Sutcliffe started work as a truck driver. This allowed him to move around undetected through a larger area of Yorkshire. During this time, until his arrest in 1981, Sutcliffe carried out most of his brutal attacks and murders. Yet, to the outside world, he was a trusted employee and regular guy just living his life.

"It's all right, I know what you're leading up to. **THE YORKSHIRE RIPPER.** *It's* **ME.** *I* **KILLED** *all those* **WOMEN."**

—PETER SUTCLIFFE

METHODS AND MOTIVES

Between 1975 and 1980, Sutcliffe murdered at least 13 women and brutally attacked 8 others, who survived with severe injuries and lasting trauma. Not all his victims are known, but it is thought that he began assaulting (and possibly killing) women in the late 1960s.

Sutcliffe mainly targeted sex workers because he saw them as easy victims who probably wouldn't be missed, and he knew the police wouldn't prioritize their deaths. He viciously battered his victims with a hammer, or stabbed and mutilated them with a knife or screwdriver. Some were strangled with rope.

Sutcliffe's true motives aren't known, but when he was caught, he said he had killed sex workers because he believed he was on a divine mission to rid the world of prostitutes. However, some of his victims weren't sex workers—he also killed several students, a bank teller, and a civil servant. Some people believe he was a misogynist and that he murdered his victims to satisfy his own depraved needs.

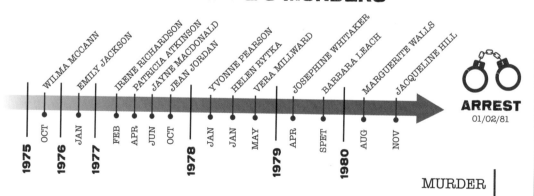

TIMELINE OF SUTCLIFFE'S MURDERS

WILMA MCCANN — OCT 1975
EMILY JACKSON — JAN 1976
IRENE RICHARDSON — FEB 1977
PATRICIA ATKINSON — APR.
JAYNE MACDONALD — JUN
JEAN JORDAN — OCT
YVONNE PEARSON — JAN 1978
HELEN RYTKA — JAN
VERA MILLWARD — MAY
JOSEPHINE WHITAKER — APR. 1979
BARBARA LEACH — SPET
MARGUERITE WALLS — AUG 1980
JACQUELINE HILL — NOV

ARREST
01/02/81

MURDER

CAPTURE AND TRIAL

As the number of suspected victims of the Yorkshire Ripper rose and fear spread across northern England, the police started advising women to stay home at night or to only go out with a trusted male escort. In a yearlong manhunt, and over 2.5 million hours of police work, some serious errors were made and vital evidence was missed. There were no computers to cross-reference all the information gathered. A hoax tape, purportedly sent from the Ripper, led investigators down the wrong path. Sutcliffe had a Yorkshire accent, confirmed by some of his surviving victims, but the voice on the tape didn't, so the police started looking outside Yorkshire, during which time Sutcliffe killed three more women. Sutcliffe was even interviewed nine times before he was caught.

Finally, on January 2, 1981, Sutcliffe was arrested in Sheffield. He was sitting in a car with a sex worker, Olivia Reivers, when police spotted his fake license plates. They found screwdrivers in his car, and a hammer and knife near the scene of his arrest. Sutcliffe was taken into custody where he confessed to the crimes.

During his trial, Sutcliffe pleaded guilty to manslaughter, not murder, claiming diminished responsibility. On May 22, 1981, he was found guilty of 13 murders and 7 counts of attempted murder. He was given 20 life sentences, with a minimum sentence of 30 years.

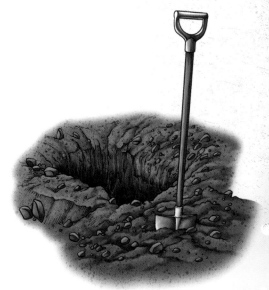

In 1984, Sutcliffe was diagnosed with paranoid schizophrenia, and he was sent to Broadmoor Hospital, a secure psychiatric facility. He applied for the right to parole, but this was denied. In 2016, he was declared mentally fit and was sent to a maximum-security prison to serve out the rest of his sentence.

DEATH

On November 13, 2020, Sutcliffe died at University Hospital, North Durham, where he was being treated for a suspected heart attack. He had also tested positive for Covid-19 but had refused treatment for it.

FRED & ROSE WEST

THE YOUNG FRED WEST

Fred West was born into poverty and incest. While his father was abusing West's three younger sisters, along with other young girls, his mother abused him. It is thought that West also raped one of his sisters when he was 20 years old. West didn't do well at school and dropped out. He worked as a farm laborer, in a slaughterhouse, and was, at one point, an ice cream man. After two work-related accidents left him with serious head injuries, which may have affected his behavior and impulse control, West began a life of petty crime. He was known to the police and was convicted of child molestation on many occasions.

THE YOUNG ROSE WEST

Rose Letts was also a victim of incest by her father, who was a paranoid schizophrenic with violent behavior. Her mother lived with mental illness too and she had received electroconvulsion therapy during her pregnancy with Letts, which could have affected her development. Letts was aggressive and suffered with weight problems. She didn't do well at school, and from a young age she found she was attracted to older men. Her parents soon divorced. Letts left with her mother but at 15 years old, she'd started dating West and subsequently moved back in with her father.

A DEADLY MATCH

By the time West and Letts got married, West already had a stepdaughter, Charmaine, and daughter Anne Marie from his first marriage to a woman named Catherine Costello, and he and Rose had a daughter named Heather. Mrs. West then started to sell herself for sex, and both she and West had casual sex with the lodgers in their house. The couple went on to have four more children together, and Rose had a further three children with one of her sex clients. Following in the horrific footsteps of both their own childhood traumas, the Wests beat, tortured, and sexually abused some of their own children.

"*Now the thing that makes it* **HARD***, is that she [Rose]* **CUT HEATHER UP***, and chucked her in a* **DUSTBIN***.*"
—FRED WEST

METHODS AND MOTIVES

The couple carried out their barbaric assault and killing spree for 20 years between 1967 and 1987, killing at least 12 women and young girls, including their own daughters Charmaine, age 8, and Heather, age 16, and West's first wife Costello.

The deeply disturbed couple, as victims of childhood abuse themselves, saw no wrong in their actions. They preyed on vulnerable girls and women to play out their warped sexual fantasies. Violent and remorseless, they evolved into brutal, coldblooded killers.

In a cellar in their home that they had fitted out as a bondage chamber, they raped and tortured their victims before murdering them. They would then dismember their bodies and bury them. Mr. West would cut off their fingers and toes, in what would become his signature M.O.

When their depraved crimes were finally unearthed, the bodies of nine of their victims were found buried at 25 Cromwell Road, their home that became infamously known as the "House of Horrors."

CAPTURE AND TRIAL

In August 1992, an investigation was launched into the couple. The police discovered that two of their older daughters, Charmaine and Heather, had disappeared. The Wests said the girls had run away, and the other children were coerced by their parents not to say anything. The case against them eventually collapsed when key witnesses said they wouldn't testify against the Wests.

The police continued to search for the missing daughters. Finally, in 1994, with evidence stacking up against them, a warrant was issued to search the Wests' house and land. As more and more bodies were found, Fred admitted to the murders, claiming sole responsibility. Rose was released on bail, but later rearrested when her role in the grisly murders became apparent.

Fred was charged with 12 counts of first-degree murder and appeared in court for the final time before his death on December 13, 1994. Rose eventually received a life sentence without the possibility of parole in November 1995.

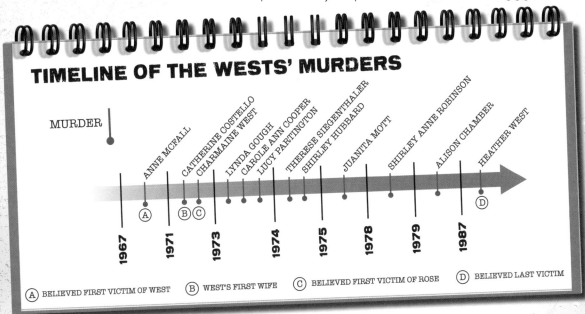

TIMELINE OF THE WESTS' MURDERS

MURDER

ANNE MCFALL
CATHERINE COSTELLO
CHARMAINE WEST
LYNDA GOUGH
CAROLE ANN COOPER
LUCY PARTINGTON
THERESE SIEGENTHALER
SHIRLEY HUBBARD
JUANITA MOTT
SHIRLEY ANNE ROBINSON
ALISON CHAMBER
HEATHER WEST

1967   1971   1973   1974   1975   1978   1979   1987

(A) BELIEVED FIRST VICTIM OF WEST   (B) WEST'S FIRST WIFE   (C) BELIEVED FIRST VICTIM OF ROSE   (D) BELIEVED LAST VICTIM

DEATH

On January 1, 1995, Fred West was found hanged in his cell while he was being held in custody at HMP Birmingham, England, before he could be sentenced for his harrowing crimes. Rose is currently still serving her sentence at HMP New Hall, in West Yorkshire, England.

AILEEN WUORNOS

SENTENCED TO DEATH · SENTENCED TO DEATH · SENTENCE TO DEATH · SENTENCED TO DEATH ·

THE YOUNG WUORNOS

Born to teenage parents, Aileen Wuornos was the victim of child abuse. Her mother abandoned her and her siblings when she was just four years old, and she was left in the care of her maternal grandparents, who were alcoholics. Her father was jailed for raping a minor, and he committed suicide in prison when she was 13 years old.

Wuornos was beaten and sexually abused by her grandfather and some of his friends, and she committed incest with her brother Keith, who was one year older than her. When she became pregnant at the age of 15, after being raped by a family friend, Wuornos was forced to give her child up for adoption and was driven out of her home. This was to be the start of a life littered with minor offenses. She lived rough in the woods and turned to the sex trade to earn money for food.

When Wuornos was 20, she tried to escape her troubled life by moving to Florida and marrying a much older, wealthy man, but she struggled to stay away from petty crime and the marriage was annulled after just nine weeks. During the 1980s, Wuornos was regularly in trouble with the police for various crimes, from prostitution to car theft, assault, and armed robbery.
In 1986, she met and fell in love with a woman named Tyria Moore. Moore was a motel maid in Daytona Beach. They moved in together and Wuornos tried to support Moore with the money she earned from her sex work.

METHODS AND MOTIVES

It is perhaps not surprising, given her traumatic childhood, that the deeply disturbed Wuornos went on to become America's first confirmed female serial killer. She carried out her brutal murders along Florida's highways in late 1989 and 1990, where she shot dead at least six men.

Pretending to hitchhike, Wuornos would flag down the men and offer them sex. She would then shoot them dead, steal their possessions, and dump their naked bodies in remote wooded areas along Florida's highways.

On November 30, 1989, Wuornos killed her first victim, 51-year-old Richard Mallory. His body was found two weeks later in woods off the highway, riddled with bullets. Over the next year, she murdered five more men. It is also believed that she killed Peter Siems, who disappeared in June 1990, but his body has never been found. After she was caught, Wuornos claimed that she killed the men in self-defense when they became violent toward her, but later admitted that she killed for profit.

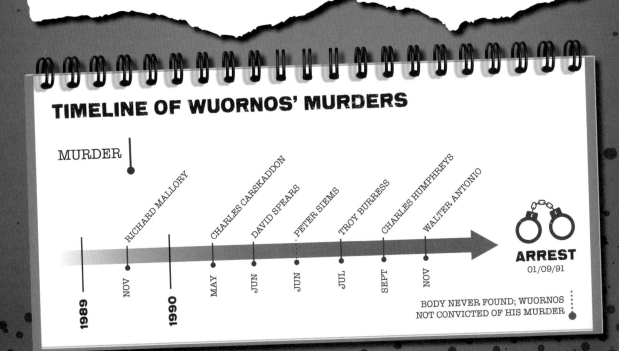

TIMELINE OF WUORNOS' MURDERS

MURDER

RICHARD MALLORY

CHARLES CARSKADDON

DAVID SPEARS

PETER SIEMS

TROY BURRESS

CHARLES HUMPHREYS

WALTER ANTONIO

ARREST
01/09/91

1989   NOV   1990   MAY   JUN   JUN   JUL   SEPT   NOV

BODY NEVER FOUND; WUORNOS
NOT CONVICTED OF HIS MURDER

CAPTURE AND TRIAL

Wuornos' killing spree came to a halt when Peter Siems' car was found at the end of 1990, crashed along a roadside. Her fingerprints were found in the car and on items belonging to Siems that were recovered from a local pawn shop. The police tracked down Wuornos and on January 9, 1991, they arrested her at a biker's bar in Port Orange, Florida. The next day, they arrested Moore, who had fled to Pennsylvania.

Moore was persuaded to trick Wuornos into confessing to the murders in a taped phone call, and was given full immunity for her cooperation.

During her trial, the defense claimed that Wuornos was mentally unstable and that she could be suffering from borderline personality disorder. These claims were dismissed, and on January 27, 1992, Wuornos was convicted of Mallory's murder and sentenced to death. On the March 31, 1992, she received three more death sentences for the murders of David Spears, Troy Burress, and Charles Humphreys. She later pleaded guilty to the murders of Charles Carskaddon and Walter Antonio, and was given a further two death sentences. As Siems' body was never found, Wuornos was not charged with his murder.

> *"I am as* **GUILTY** *as can be. I want the world to know* **I KILLED THESE MEN, AS COLD AS ICE.** *I've* **HATED HUMANS** *for a long time. I am a serial killer.* **I KILLED THEM IN COLD BLOOD,** *real nasty."*
> —AILEEN WUORNOS

Wuornos was executed by lethal injection on October 9, 2002, after spending a decade on death row at the Florida Department of Corrections' Broward Correctional Institution. She was transferred to Florida State Prison for her execution.

YOO YOUNG-CHUL

CRIMINAL PROFILE:

Name: Yoo Young-chul
Date of birth: April 18, 1970
Place of birth: Gochang County, Jeonbuk, South Korea.
Also known as: The Raincoat Killer
Victims: At least 20
Convicted: Sentenced to death

THE YOUNG YOO YOUNG-CHUL

Yoo Young-chul grew up in poverty. His parents separated a few years after he was born and he moved to Seoul with his father. Young-chul was bullied at school. He resented his impoverished life and fostered a lifetime hatred and jealousy of the wealthy, rich, and privileged.

Between 1988 and 2000, Young-chul lived a life of petty crime. He married in 1991 and had a son, but spent many months in and out of prison charged with theft, selling child pornography, and for forgery and fraud. His crimes took an even darker turn when he raped a 15-year-old girl in 2000. Young-chul was sentenced to three years and six months in prison, and his wife subsequently divorced him.

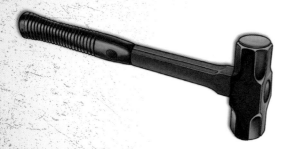

After his release from prison in September 2003, Young-chul began his appalling killing spree. He murdered at least 20 people, making him the deadliest serial killer in South Korean history.

"I did it to KILL SOCIETY."

—YOO YOUNG-CHUL

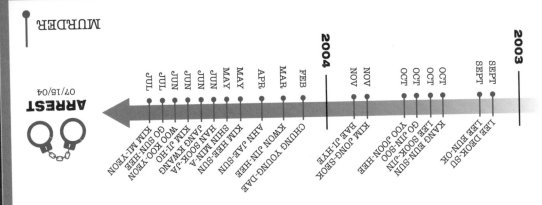

TIMELINE OF YOUNG-CHUL'S MURDERS

2003
- SEPT — LEE DEOK-SU
- SEPT — KANG EUN-SUN
- OCT — LEE EUN-SUN
- OCT — GO JIN-SOO
- OCT — YOO JOON-SOO
- NOV — KIM JONG-SEOK
- NOV — BAE JI-HYE

2004
- FEB — CHUNG YOUNG-DAE
- MAR — KWON JIN-HEE
- APR — AHN JAE-SUN
- MAY — KIM HEE-SUN
- MAY — SHIN MIN-A
- JUN — HAN HEE-SUN
- JUN — JANG KWANG
- JUN — KIM JI-HO
- JUL — WOO EUN-YEON
- JUL — GO SUN-HEE
- JUL — KIM MI-YEON

ARREST 07/15/04

MURDER

METHODS AND MOTIVES

It was while he was in prison that Young-chul began to plan his first murder. He read about the Korean serial killer Jeong Du-yeong, who had targeted rich people as his victims. With his own resentment of the wealth divide in South Korea, and his newfound hatred of women post-divorce, Young-chul settled on his target: rich women—and any men that got in his way.

On September 24, 2003, he carried out his first murders. He broke into the home of a university professor and his wife, then stabbed the professor and beat his wife to death with a custom-made sledgehammer. In a frenzied spree, Young-chul went on to kill six more people over the next two months, and later admitted he ate some of their livers.

It was during this time that he started dating an escort girl, but when she discovered he had a criminal record, she left him. Young-chul's hatred for women escalated, and he channeled his anger onto sex workers. Changing his M.O., Young-chul would invite sex workers from the Seoul massage parlors to his apartment, where he bludgeoned them to death with his sledgehammer.

DEATH

On December 13, 2004, Young-chul was convicted of 20 first-degree murders and sentenced to death.